Fishing for Fun

A Freshwater Guide

by Charles P. Roberts
and George F. Roberts

Dillon Press, Inc.   Minneapolis, Minnesota   55415

Library of Congress Cataloging in Publication Data

Roberts, Charles P.
  Fishing for fun

  Includes index.
  (Doing and learning books)
  Summary: Introduces the beginning fisherman to
equipment, bait, lures, and knots, and explains where
and when to fish, and how to clean fish, emphasizing
simple and inexpensive approaches to the sport.
  1. Fishing—Juvenile literature. [1. Fishing]
I. Roberts, George F. II. Title. III. Series.
SH445.R63   1984   799.1'1   83-23239
ISBN 0-87518-252-6

Dillon Press, Inc., 242 Portland Avenue South
Minneapolis, Minnesota 55415

Printed in the United States of America
  2 3 4 5 6 7 8 9 10 92 91 90 89 88 87 86 85

The photographs are reproduced through the courtesy of Charles P. Roberts, George F. Roberts, Joseph N. Roberts, the Wisconsin Department of Natural Resources, and Dr. Bill Schmid, University of Minnesota.

The illustrations were done by George F. Roberts.

The original fish paintings were done by Virgil Beck.

Contents

Acknowledgments

We are especially grateful to our friend and neighbor Dare Kibble for telling us the delightful stories of his youth that gave this book its form and rhythm.

We would also like to thank the following friends for their stories and ideas: Jim Maguire, Dale Crammer, and Jack Rorer.

We are indebted to our parents and George's wife, Susan, for their suggestions and criticism of the manuscript. A special thanks, also, to our brothers, especially John—that militant non-fisherman, for their corrections and additions that were most helpful in keeping us on the right track.

Finally, we would like to thank our Mom for taking so much time from her busy life to type the final draft.

Fishing from a horse is just one way to enjoy fishing.

CHAPTER 1

Getting Started

At last the rush of Nip-n-Tuck Creek could be heard above the buzzing insects and the steady clopping of the horse's hooves. Dare didn't need to urge the mare. The smell of water was enough to start her trotting. Horse and rider moved through the heavy heat and dry brush to the cool air that flowed with the creek. The thought of the sleek fish swimming in the creek made Dare smile with pleasure.

As the horse drank from the clear, cool water, Dare leaned over and cut a sturdy willow branch to use as a fishing pole. From a leather pouch in his hip pocket, he took a coil of line, a hook, a tiny lead ball, and a dead grasshopper. He tied the line to the leafy end of the branch. To the other end of the line he attached the hook with the grasshopper stuck on it. Above the hook he pinched on the piece of lead for weight.

As Dare worked, his horse splashed to midstream. Dare watched as the startled trout darted about in the clear water, then quickly calmed down. These fish had seen too many cattle to be bothered much by a single horse. Dare lazily lay back on the animal's broad rump and let his line wind with the current into the water above the fish. At first the trout ignored the tumbling grasshopper. But before long a hungry trout took a bite of the bait. Dare pulled back against the fighting fish, which bent and bounced his pole. Tiring from the fight, the trout made a final leap to shake loose. It wasn't enough. Dare pulled the fish out of the water, grabbing it with his free hand as it bounced against the horse's side.

Now that's fishing! Using simple but basic fishing skills and equipment, Dare was able to fool a trout into biting his hook. But Dare was not always a good angler.* He used to approach the sport like most beginners. He felt he needed the best equipment—fishing rod and reel, invisible line, and a tackle box full of lures and gadgets— just to get started. He learned this was not true from a man named Pierpont Desire Noulton.

Pont, short for Pierpont, was a friend of Dare's father. Pont owned a cattle ranch in the Owyhee Mountains of southern Idaho where Dare worked each summer. Dare loved everything about ranch life, especially fishing.

During Dare's first summer at the ranch, he learned a lesson in fishing he never forgot. Some people from the city hired Pont to guide them on a fishing trip. According to Pont, each of the guests was a good angler. When the guests arrived, Dare admired their expensive equipment. Later Pont showed everyone the equipment he intended

*A person who goes fishing has traditionally been called a fisherman. In this book the term angler is used, since both boys and girls, and men and women, can enjoy this sport.

to use—nothing more than a bit of line, some hooks, lead weight, and a willow pole. Everyone laughed, thinking it was a joke.

The next day Pont placed each person at a spot on the river where he knew the fishing would be excellent. Once the visitors started fishing, Pont wandered farther downstream with just his simple fishing gear.

Dare spent his time watching the guests, hoping to learn from these anglers with the beautiful gear. The day passed quickly, and each person caught plenty of fish. Dare was impressed at the size of some of the fish. Pont hadn't been seen since morning, and Dare began to feel sorry for him with his little gear. Just then Pont appeared with a gunnysack full of the biggest fish Dare had ever seen. Dare was lucky to learn so early that there is a big difference between having good equipment and being a good angler. Pont never owned any other gear. He didn't need to, and neither do you.

Let's take another look at the equipment Pont used: fishing hooks, about twenty feet of fishing line, a couple of lead weights, or split shot, and that's all. The hooks should be fairly small, one-half to three-fourths inch long. The weights can be small or large, but small is preferred. The fishing line should be nylon and at least 4 pound test. That means it will hold four pounds without breaking. A four-pound fish is a big fish.

The easiest way to get your gear is to buy it. If you have a job, you'll have the cash. But if you don't, you'll need other means.

The other means and the cheapest is to find your necessary pieces of equipment. Fishing hooks often get caught in snags, and many anglers, for the sake of convenience, will break their line in order to go on fishing. You can find lost equipment by looking along the edge of lakes and rivers. Sometime you might have come across someone's lost gear and didn't even know it. Have you ever been wading or playing in water and suddenly found your toes and legs in the clutches of a tentacled monster? And did you discover to your relief that it was only a piece of nylon fishing line? This is an example of lost equipment you can use.

The best time to go hunting for lost gear is in the summer when waters are low or receding. The first thing you will probably spot is fishing line. When you find it, work your way carefully along the line in both directions. Take care not to follow the line blindly into deep water. At the end of the line, you may find hooks, weights, even lures. Of course, you may not find any of these things the first try. But, at least, you will have the line. Wind the line on a stick, put it in your pocket, and go on searching.

Most fishing line is nylon. If left in the sun too long, nylon will become stiff. Test the line by pulling hard on it. If the line stretches, as nylon should, you have a good piece. If it is stiff or breaks, throw it away in a trash can. There will be better line farther up the shore. Twenty feet of good line will do to begin with. You can even tie several smaller pieces together (see Appendix: Knots).

Hooks are almost always found attached to fishing line. Therefore, you should pick up every piece of line you come across. The hooks may appear rusted. Keep them anyway. Scrape a rusty hook with a knife or use an emery board (a nail file made of cardboard and covered with a coarse powder) to remove all the rust. If the rust is deep, throw the hook away safely. If you have found only one hook, you have enough.

Sinkers, or weights, can be found attached to the line, as well. Sinkers are made of lead and are almost always reusable. Usually they are attached to the line near the hook.

There are two basic types of sinkers. With the first, the line is tied to the sinker. This kind you just cut loose. The other, called split shot, is attached to the line by biting and needs to have its mouth reopened to be removed. To do this, stick a knife blade into the crack that encloses the line and pull it open, figure 1-1. The split shot should fall off.

Fig. 1-1

Remember, line, hook, and sinker were all that Pont needed. This is also what you will usually find. But you may find other things as well. Especially watch for bobbers, lures, and swivels. These items are all lying out there waiting to be claimed and are almost always attached to fishing line. Don't count on completely outfitting yourself this way. Chapters 3 and 5 cover more equipment that can be made or inexpensively purchased to help complete your kit.

Now that you have your equipment, are you ready to fish? The answer is—not quite. You will also need bait. Remember the grasshopper Dare used? That is what is called bait or the food fish eat. As a beginning angler, use the common earthworm. It is the oldest, most widely known, and best of the baits.

Worms prefer rich, damp ground in a cool, shady area. Dig in a choice bit of garden soil, a well-worked flower bed, a manure pile, or leafy ground. Dig up a shovelful of dirt, and carefully sift through it, breaking the clods and watching for the wigglers. You may have to dig up a large area to find enough worms. If digging does not yield many, hose down your lawn or wait until after a rain. Worms need air, too, and the water drives them to the surface. After such a soaking, go out searching at night with a flashlight. This should yield a sufficient harvest.

Once you have a dozen or more worms, you'll have to keep them somewhere. For best results, put the worms in a container, such as an empty cottage cheese carton, filled with moist dirt. You will need a lid to keep your worms from crawling away. Poke holes in the lid so the worms can breathe and keep their strength. An old wool sock will work, too, as long as it has no holes for the worms to escape through. Put some damp dirt in the sock with your worms.

Dead worms make bad bait, and they stink. If you are not going fishing right away, keep the container of worms cool, moist, and out of the sun. The refrigerator is a good place to keep them, but first make certain your parents don't mind. Sneaking them in could delay your fishing indefinitely.

With pockets full of equipment and worms in hand, it is time to go fishing. The big question is where to fish? Even in a large city, you might find a park with a pond or a golf course. If there is a golf course near your home, ask the manager for permission to fish the course pond. Golf course ponds are often filled with bass, bluegill, and catfish and are excellent places to begin to learn the joys of fishing.

If there are no parks or golf courses nearby, get hold of a map of your area. Look for little blue blobs on it. The blue areas indicate lakes or ponds. Squiggly blue lines represent rivers or streams. Find your house on the map, and trace your way to the water you have chosen. In chapter 2 you will find many more ways of discovering a fishing hole.

Now you are ready to go fishing. Drag yourself out of bed early. Don't complain. Enjoy the brisk air and the chirping birds. Most of all, think of catching those hungry fish. Don't forget your friend, even if it is very early in the morning. A partner is not only a help when in trouble, but a friend can also be a witness to that huge fish that got away!

When you arrive at your fishing spot, choose a small-sized hook, one that is about one-half inch long. The hook must be small enough to enter the fish's mouth but large enough to hook its lip. Now tie the hook to the end of the line (see Appendix: Knots).

A split shot or other sinker should be attached about twelve inches above the hook. This helps you to throw the bait far out into the water, as well as to sink the worm to the bottom. Never put a sinker too close to the hook. It will only frighten the fish when it nibbles the bait.

Fig. 1-2

One of the more ticklish problems for a beginner is baiting the hook. The idea is to hide as much of the hook from the fish as possible. All you want the fish to see is your bait. You also want to avoid killing your bait when you hook it. Lively bait catches more fish.

To bait your hook, take out a wiggly worm and stick its front end on the hook, figure 1-2. You'll know the front end by the direction the worm crawls. Keep threading the worm on until the hook is entirely covered. Of course, the worm will not cooperate. It will wiggle and squirm to pull itself from between your fingers. A worm seems to be the most difficult to handle when everyone else is catching fish, and you are in a hurry to join them. Never let a worm get the best of you. If you can't thread the wiggler head first, stick it on any way you can. Just pierce the hook through the worm's body in two or three places so it ends up all bunched on the hook, figure 1-3. In fact, that's the only way you can bait small worms.

Now everything is rigged and ready to go. The next step is to throw the bait out to the fish. The throwing, or casting, must be done without hooking yourself, your friend, your dog, or a tree.

There are two different ways to cast your hand line, depending on shore conditions. For best results, practice both in your backyard before going fishing so you can avoid mistakes.

One casting method is used when the shore is free of low branches and thick brush. String your line in one large loop on the water's edge, figure 1-4. Holding the end

Fig. 1-3

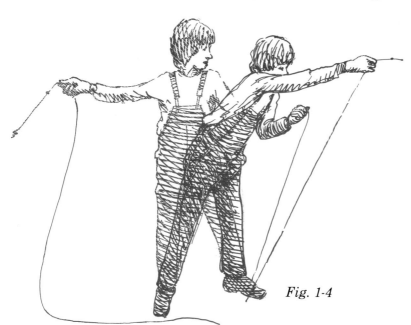

Fig. 1-4

firmly in one hand, grab the line above the weight with the other. Using an underhand swing, throw your bait out into the water.

If the shore is too rocky or brush covered to lay the line out, a different technique is used. Tie the line one inch from the end of a six-inch long fat, smooth stick. Wrap the line towards the short end, leaving the hook and weight hanging, figure 1-5. Hold the long end of the stick in your palm with your thumb over the coiled line. This will keep the line from winding off before you cast, figure 1-6. Swing the stick underhand, releasing your thumb at the same time, figure 1-7. If the line is wrapped

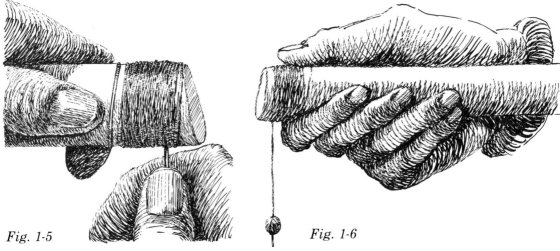

Fig. 1-5   Fig. 1-6

neatly on the stick, it should spin off nicely. Always release the line as it swings forward to be sure that it flies outward, instead of upward or backward where fish do not live. Be sure to tie the line firmly to the stick so you

Fig. 1-7

won't throw your fishing gear away. In an article in *Ranger Rick's Nature Magazine*, Edward Matthews suggests using an aluminum pop can instead of a stick. A can also works very well.

Once you have cast out your line, the sinker will pull the line and bait to the bottom. This kind of fishing is called bottom fishing. Keep the line tight to feel the fish nibbling at your worm. Don't leave your line unattended, or the fish will make off with everything.

When you feel a slight tugging, a fish is biting. Give the line a quick yank back. Don't pull too hard, or you might pull the hook right out of the fish's mouth. If the line responds with a tug and resists, hold on to your hat—you've hooked a fish.

Bring in the fish, using a steady hand-over-hand retrieve. Enjoy the fun of feeling a fish fighting on your line. Don't be in a hurry to pull the fish in because it puts too much strain on your hand line. Once the fish is tired, drag it on shore quickly. If you are on a high bank, dock,

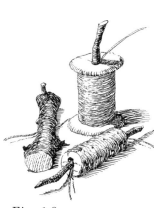

Fig. 1-8

Fig. 1-9

bridge, or horse, you have no choice but to pull the fish out of the water while it is still dangling on the end of your line. By being quick and smooth, you can avoid losing the fish. Once on shore, the fish can still get away, so tackle and wrestle your fish as soon as it hits land.

If after five minutes you still feel no bites, pull in your line to check the bait. If your worm is gone, some fish may have stolen it. There is nothing to do but put a fresh worm on your hook and cast to the same spot. Maybe this time you'll catch the thief.

Many times, however, your worm will still be on the hook when you bring it in. This means that there are probably no fish in that spot. When this happens, walk down the shore a ways and cast in an entirely new spot. By doing so, you will soon find the hole where the fish are feeding.

If after half an hour of bottom fishing you still have had no luck, it's time to try bobber fishing. Depending on the type of fish, the time of day, and the food, a fish will feed at different levels in the water and not just on the bottom. Bobber fishing allows you to fish at different depths and, thus, fish where the fish are feeding.

To bobber fish you need something that floats. Tie a small stick, an empty thread spool, a bottle cork, or a store-bought bobber to your line above the sinker, figure 1-8. Do not tie the bobber so far above the sinker that you cannot swing the line while casting. The float holds the bait as deep as the distance from the bobber to the hook, figure 1-9. Watch the float carefully. If the float begins to bob or move about unexpectedly, a fish is taking the bait. Give the line a quick yank. This often hooks the fish. Sometimes, however, you will find you do not have a fish. When this happens, the fish is just playing with its food. That's bad manners. To teach the fish a lesson, be patient until it is ready to eat and pulls the bobber entirely underwater. Then you have hooked the fish.

Once you have landed the fish, it must be put somewhere before you can continue to fish. Your back pocket won't do, so put your catch in a bucket of water to keep it fresh. You can also put your catch on a stringer. A stringer is a handy piece of string that works like a dog leash. Poke the string through the fish's gills and out its mouth. Then tie the string together near the fish. Attach the other end securely to something on shore so the fish cannot swim away. This will keep the fish alive in the water while you continue fishing. You will learn more about stringers in chapter 3.

When you go home to show off your fish, everyone will want to eat them. First they must be cleaned. The fish must be cut open, the insides removed, and the bloodline scraped out. The scales must then be scraped off, and the fish washed in water before it is cooked. Chapter 8 will elaborate on this messy business.

So there you have it, a beginning. Like Pont and Dare, you can catch a fish using just a hook, line, and sinker. Dare always carried his little fishing kit with him so that while he was tending trap lines or herding cattle he could fish. You can, too. Just wrap the line around a two-by-six-inch piece of cardboard, and stick the hooks into it, figure 1-10. Fold the cardboard in half, and put it in your pocket along with the sinkers. Now you are ready for any fishing opportunity that comes your way—whether you're walking home from school, out on a hike, or in the car with your parents. Just pull out your hook wallet, find some bait, and fish to your heart's content.

There is much more to learn if you want to be a good angler like Pont and Dare. They always knew when and where to fish and when and where not to fish. You need to learn that as well. The next chapter will help you find out where to fish.

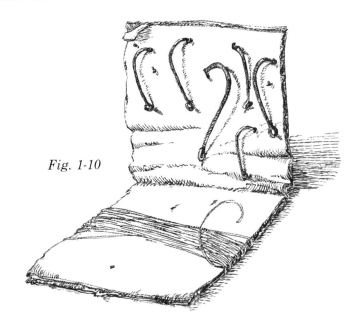

Fig. 1-10

CHAPTER 2
Where to Fish

To discover a new fishing spot is exciting. Yet finding a new place to fish can be one of the more difficult features of fishing. This is especially true when you are first venturing out into the fishing world.

The first thing is to know what you are looking for; the next step is to know where and how to look. A pond is a good place to start. There are so many ponds around that, at least, one can be found near your home. Ponds come in a variety of forms with as great a variety of fish living in them. Because they are small, you can get to know every rock, snag, and hot spot on them. Soon they will become as familiar to you as your own backyard.

The farm pond is used for irrigation, watering livestock, raising ducks, and for fishing. Abandoned sand and gravel pits can be great fishing spots as well. You must take care around them because the sides are often slippery and steep. Old abandoned rock quarries will often fill with water and are sometimes so clear you can see the fish swimming in them.

There are all kinds of natural ponds, such as beaver, bog, and cypress ponds. There are also many ponds that have no name—just holes in the ground filled with water and fish.

Most ponds are privately owned. Ask permission before you go fishing in someone's pond. And, while there, be the kind of person who will be invited back.

There are other kinds of still water that are not privately owned. Large, slow-moving rivers often spread to form backwater, sloughs, and bayous. Fish love these shallow bodies of water, which are often covered with plants and litter. Some backwaters are so shallow and polluted that only air-sucking carp can live in them. But most are fine, warm water fisheries with granddaddy fish waiting to be caught.

Lakes are very popular spots when you want to fish still water. They can be measured in square miles like the huge Great Lakes, or they can be as small as ponds, such as the high mountain lakes of the West. They can be very deep like the seemingly bottomless Crater Lake or as shallow as the famous bass lakes in the South. It's just plain hard not to live near a lake or reservoir, and usually it's easy to find public routes to them.

Your fishing opportunities don't stop here, either. There are plenty of freshwater fish in moving water. Rivers, streams, creeks, canals, and ditches are moving water, and all are easy to recognize. They are a delight to see, hear, and smell. Most of all, they are a joy to fish.

Rivers range from those that flow slowly through flat country to cold, clear, rocky streams that rush down the mountains. No two streams are exactly alike. Each has its own charms and its own kind of fishing.

Knowing what to look for only solves half the problem. Knowing how and where to find a pond or creek is the other half. The best place to start is with your state fish and game authority. They should be able to answer most of your questions, even give you maps and directions. Look them up in the telephone book under the name of your state. Depending on where you live, the fishing division could be listed under a variety of departments. The following departments are the most common in the United States: conservation, natural resources, environmental protection or management, parks and wildlife, and fish and game. Call and ask for information about local fishing. You will want to know where there's a good fishing spot near your home. Describe what you have in the way of equipment and the available bait. This information will help your state agency to steer you to some good fishing.

Don't forget to ask your local fish and game authority about the fishing regulations. You may be old enough to need a fishing license. You should also ask when waters are open for legal fishing, and how many fish you can keep. All of these regulations are necessary to insure that there will be good fishing from one year to the next and for generations to come. So consult the fish and game officer, obey the regulations, and help maintain good fishing in your area. Remember, even if you are not old enough to need a license, the same rules and regulations apply.

Fishing shops and sporting goods stores can also be

good sources of information about local fishing. Politely ask the shopkeeper to direct you to the good, local fishing spots.

If you still need more information, there are fishing clubs to consult and join. You can ask about these organizations at the fishing shops or by contacting your state fish and game authority. Attend the meetings, and listen carefully to the talk of the experienced anglers. Join them in their conservation efforts and club projects. You will not only enjoy yourself but gain life-long friends, as well as loads of fishing tales and good advice.

Many local newspapers publish information about fishing in the area, including fishing conditions at a particular time. Usually this informaton will be provided once a week in the sports section of your local newspaper, figure 2-1.

If nothing else works, get a detailed, up-to-date county map. Most county maps will show rivers and lakes as well as roads. Lay the map out on the table, and study the bodies of water that look worth investigating. Study the map very carefully because some maps don't distinguish between public and private roads. Other maps sometimes show roads that are only proposed but either not begun or not yet completed. Following these maps can lead you on a merry chase from pavement, to dirt, to quicksand. A great adventure can be discovered, which can lead to some very exciting fishing.

Finally, an excellent source of information is your fellow angler. Another angler will understand your needs because it is the duty of all anglers to constantly search for new waters. If you see someone walking with a stringer of fine, fat fish and you don't ask where they were caught, you have yet to catch the spirit of the sport. However, the subject should be approached indirectly. Beat around the bush for awhile before approaching the subject cautiously. The conversation could go something like this:

"You have some nice fish there. Get them using night crawlers?"

"Nope, red worms."

Already you have a little information and have put the other person in the mood to answer questions. Ask another innocent question such as:

Fishing report

The following outlook for the weekend and potpourri of fishing tips is provided by local fishing shops:

Fishermen can't miss if they pick the **Snake River** anywhere from C.J. Strike Reservoir to Steck Park. In Strike Reservoir anglers are picking up trout. crappie, bass and channel catfish. Jigging is the best with one 6½-pound channel cat reported taken on a Puddle Jumper spinner with a white curl-tail jig. From Swan Falls downstream, smallmouth bass and channel catfish are taking anything that looks like a crawdad. Fly fishermen have been doing especially well with a crawdad fly. From Walter's Ferry downstream, drifting for channel catfish with nightcrawlers is excellent. The Steck Park area is also good for catfish and perch . . . Smallmouths are hitting along the **Lower Payette River**. The eddies are the places to find fish. Frog-colored Flatfish, wobble spoons and spinners are the right choices in lures . . . Early-bird anglers who manage to be on **Lake Lowell** by 5:30 a.m. and who are willing to fight the jungle weed on the edge of the lake, can find hawg largemouth bass. Bluegills also are hitting near the dams. Use a nightcrawler/bobber combination . . . Largemouth bass won't quit at **Bruneau Sand Dunes** lakes. One fisherman took bass 3½ to 5 pounds on a motor-oil colored twist tail grub on 1/8-ounce jig head. **Paddock Reservoir** has stabilized for crappies and is nothing is exceptional. Anglers are averaging 15 to 20 keepers per trip . . . the **Boise River** through Boise has been good fishing to catchable trout, 10 to 12 inches in length.

Reprinted with permission of the *Idaho Statesman*

Fig. 2-1

"Oh yeah, fish really go for those red worms on the bottom, don't they?"

"Bottom, nothing. I had them about two feet under a bobber."

Your questions are working. Now inch a little closer.

"Two feet under, you say. You must have been fishing that deep stretch below the log jam."

"The log jam is all washed out."

A false move; the stranger is catching on.

"Yeah but..." Careful now; don't blow it. "I caught a bunch of fish nearly that nice out toward Luna Lake just last week."

"Oh? I never could catch anything there."

At this point, the angler will either walk away, or will give you a little more information—maybe in exchange for a little from you. Remember, you are both anglers, and you both want the same thing—good fishing. If an angler tells everybody who asks where a good fishing spot is, it won't be good for very long. When you find your gold mine of fish, keep it to yourself. At the same time, don't be too stingy about your great spot. You were once in need of help and information yourself. Give a little to get a little, but don't give it all.

To help you remember all your good fishing spots, keep a fishing log. A log, or journal, can be made from a small, pocket, note pad. After every fishing trip, record where you fished, the date, what fish you caught, and how many. In addition, note what bait you used to catch the fish, the time of day, what kind of weather it was,

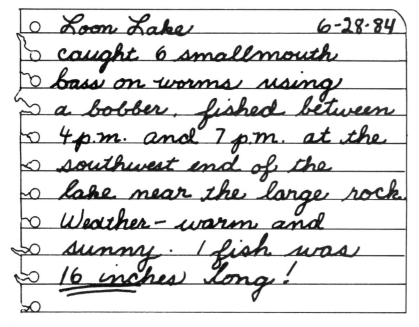

Loon Lake   6-28-84
caught 6 smallmouth
bass on worms using
a bobber. fished between
4 p.m. and 7 p.m. at the
southwest end of the
lake near the large rock.
Weather - warm and
sunny. 1 fish was
16 inches long!

Fig. 2-2

and where on the lake or river you had the best fishing, figure 2-2. Keeping all this information will make next year's fishing even better.

The more you fish, the more fishing spots you will discover. Having a good fishing partner can double the number of places. The more places you have fished, the more you will be able to exchange information with other anglers. But you won't find these places by hanging around the house. Go out and start exploring now!

CHAPTER 3

Equipment and Use

Dare's shoes squished and sloshed as he waded through the water. The sound of the creek excited Dare, and he was tempted to stop and fish. The little trout in the creek would be hungry and easy to catch. He had often fished this spot, but today Dare was going to wait until he got to the old beaver pond. The really big fish would be waiting for him there.

The rushing noise of the water grew faint as Dare moved away from the creek and pushed through the trees. A thick growth of willows and brush surrounded the beaver pond. As Dare pushed his way into the willows, he took care to hold his long cane pole behind him to keep from breaking the tip. He had not brought his spinning outfit because it would be of little use here. There was no room to cast and no room to reel in bait or fish. There were only snags to tangle his line and steal his hooks.

Finally, Dare came to the beaver pond. He could see the creek that ran smoothly into the pond and poured loudly out through a break in the old beaver dam. The pond was choked with fallen trees and weeds, but the current, which flowed along one side, formed a deep channel where the trout grew fat among the snags.

Dare found a small space on the dam where he could sit and fish. He tied three feet of line to the end of his pole. He knew a longer piece would make the cast more difficult and less accurate. Without control, he would soon find his hook caught in a snag. Next he chose a small hook and baited it with a worm. He did not use split shot because it would only be another item to snag and, in such clear water, could scare the fish.

The water was so full of fallen trees and old limbs that Dare had to place the worm carefully between the snags. He extended the pole out over a small, open area and lowered the line, quickly plopping the worm in the water. He held his pole still for a moment, waiting for a fish to bite. When nothing happened, he lowered the pole to drop the worm deeper. After a few minutes, he tried bobbing the worm up and down. Still no fish. He raised the worm out of the water and plopped it next to a log.

Suddenly a fish broke the water, took the worm, and quickly turned to the weeds where it lived. Although surprised, Dare was quicker than the fish. He held the flopping fish right at the surface. If the fish went under water, even a couple of feet, it could tangle the line and break loose. If Dare raised the fish out of the water, the fish would break the line. The fish splashed, flopped, pulled, and fought to be free. Each time the fish jumped, Dare jerked his pole a little, hopping the fish over a branch and a little closer to him. He repeated this hopping technique until the fish lay exhausted at his feet.

Had Dare not known what equipment to bring or how to use it, he might not have caught any fish and, perhaps, lost some gear in the bargain. When you are looking for new equipment, keep in mind what you need for the type of fishing you plan to do. Then learn to use the equipment. This chapter will tell you about various kinds of equipment.

Fishing Poles

One of the first items a new angler wants badly is a fishing pole. The fishing pole has two simple purposes: to get the bait out into the water and to act as a cushion to take the strain off the line while you land the fish.

Getting the bait out to the fish can be accomplished by using either a long or a short pole. A long pole, twelve to sixteen feet, can be used to extend the line and bait out over the water. A short pole, six to nine feet, is used to throw the line and bait into the water.

The long pole is ideal for certain fishing conditions. Dare's experience with the snag-infested beaver pond is one example. Bamboo or cane makes the best long pole. If you are fortunate enough to have either growing in your area, you can cut your own pole. Otherwise, many stores sell cane poles at reasonable prices. Long cane poles have been used for centuries and are still popular today. They are simple to use, but because of their unusually long length, cane poles can be awkward to handle.

Cane poles are at their best when equipped with a

short piece of fishing line, about three or four feet long, tied to the tip. On the end of this is placed a baited hook. Extend the pole out over the water, and control the depth of the bait by either raising or lowering the pole. A float can also be used and is sometimes easier than trying to hold the bait at a certain depth.

When you have a fish on the line of a cane pole, it is a mistake to lift the fish out of the water. With twelve feet of pole and only four feet of line, the fish is out of your reach and still fighting. If the shore is not thick with trees and brush, swing the pole around to the side and, backing up, drag the fish on shore. If the water's edge is lined with brush, use a hand-over-hand motion to pull the pole in while keeping the fish in the water. As with a hand line, if you are too high above the water to drag the fish in, swing the fish out of the water and on shore in one fast, smooth action.

The shorter pole is usually made from a willow branch. Hickory and hazel also make good poles, as do the branches of many other trees. Cut the branch to a length of six to nine feet with the butt about one inch thick and the tip three-eighths to one-half inch thick. Tie a piece of line, no longer than the pole, to the tip. Your cast should be the same as with the hand line, but now the length of the pole extends the distance of your cast.

When a fish is on the line, simply back away from the water, keeping the tip of the pole up to prevent the line from breaking. Continue backing up until the fish has been pulled on shore.

Fishing with your homemade pole can be fun.

A willow pole has two big advantages. First of all, you can make your own pole right at the fishing spot. And secondly, the pole won't cost you a penny.

Dare used a little secret that Pont taught him when fishing with a willow pole. He would not remove all of the little leafy branches at the end. That way the pole looked like just another tree and did not scare the fish. This can be a big advantage when you can't cast thirty yards up- or downstream.

Select your branch carefully, following these simple guidelines. For any length pole, the tip must not be too thin, or it will break easily. Test the tip for strength by bending it. It should feel firm but not require too much work to bend. On the other hand, a pole should not bend too easily. For long poles, bamboo or cane is about the best material. The short poles must have a strong butt and flexible tip. Finally, all the poles should be notched where the line is to be tied at the tip to keep the line from slipping off.

What about store-bought poles? You are, of course, interested in them, so a section has been included at the end of this chapter.

Fishing Line

If you have already found enough nylon line, you are ready to fish. If not, and you cannot afford to buy a whole spool, kite string will work. The string should be fairly thin but not so thin that it will break easily. Water rots string, so it must be treated before it can be used. The best treatment is to rub the string with wax from a candle. This will keep the line fresh and watertight. To treat the line, tie twenty-five feet of line between two trees and rub the wax in thoroughly. Leave the line out in the sun to melt the wax into the string fibers. The string will have to be rewaxed occasionally to keep it strong.

String can be seen easier than nylon fishing line, and can make the fish shy away. A dark-colored string is less visible. If your string is white, color it by rubbing the line with dark chalk before you wax it. Blue and green are good colors to use. To make the line less visible to the fish, you can also tie a short piece of nylon line on the very end of the string (see Appendix: Knots). This two- or three-foot piece of nylon line is called a leader.

Old fish are wise to the ways of anglers and may require a very fine leader to fool them into taking the bait. The only drawback is that a fine leader breaks more easily. This means the angler must take greater care to land the fish without breaking the line.

If you purchase line, 4 to 6 pound test should do for most fishing situations. You can buy heavier test line, but you'll also need a small spool of lighter, leader material.

Nylon line wrapped on a stick or spool tends to keep its curl when taken off, making it very hard to fish with. To straighten the line, pull it through a folded piece of rubber, held tightly between your fingers, figure 3-1. After every fishing trip check the line, especially the

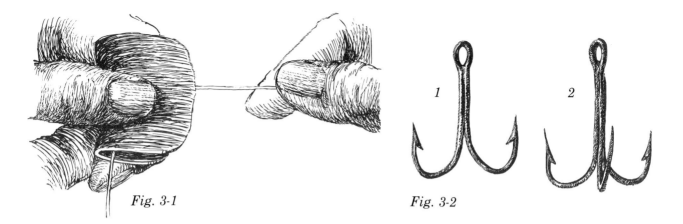

Fig. 3-1   Fig. 3-2

leader, for nicks, knots, kinks, and twists. If you find any, throw that section of line away because it is weakened and will break easily.

Hooks

The hook is one item the angler can't ignore. It holds the bait, hooks the fish, and holds the fish tight until it can be pulled to shore—no small task for such a small item. The hook also becomes a neat imitation of a fly by adding some fur and feathers. A hook looks good hanging on a hat, and it's a great relief to have one out of your ear! All in all, a hook is a mighty important little device.

In general, there are two main classes of hooks: single hooks and multiple hooks. Multiple hooks are either doubled or trebled, figure 3-2. The obvious advantage of multiple hooks is there are more points facing more directions to catch the fish and certainly more barbs to hold it. You won't be using multiple hooks for bait fishing as often as you will for lure fishing (see chapter 5). In fact, multiple hooks are often illegal for use on anything but lures.

Let's look at the single hook with a little more attention to detail. The hook is made up of an eye, the straight

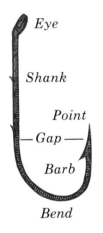

Eye

Shank

Point

— *Gap* —

Barb

Bend

Fig. 3-3

shank, the bend, the gap, and the point which carries the bite and, on some hooks, the barb, figure 3-3.

The range of sizes is tremendous, from the tiniest that can be imagined to a hook larger than your hand. Hooks ranging from one-fourth inch long to one inch or more are used in the majority of fishing situations.

Choosing the right size depends on the size of the fish and its mouth. A small hook is not as strong as a large one and, therefore, might bend or break in the mouth of a large fish. Then again, a large hook, even one inch long, might be too big for some fish's mouth and would be useless to use. But measuring hooks in inches, as we have been doing, isn't very accurate. Fortunately, hook size is numbered for fast and easy reference. Figure 3-4 shows some exact sizes you can match your hooks to and figure out what sizes you have.

For now, buy size 6, 8, or 10 hooks as a good, general, fish-catching size. A large hook, such as a size 2, is for much larger fish. Remember, the smaller the number, the larger the hook. The type of hook needed most is the bait hook. Bait hooks sometimes have a couple of barbs

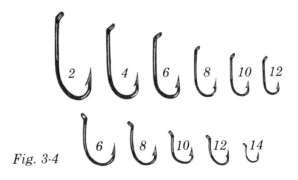

Fig. 3-4

on the shank to hold the bait, figure 3-3. Just try taking a worm off the hook, and you'll see. You can purchase bait hooks that have a short piece of leader attached. These are called snelled hooks.

Hooks with a short shank are called salmon egg hooks, figure 3-4. They are used when fishing with bait such as salmon eggs, corn kernels, and marshmallows, as well as other odd tidbits. Despite the fact that they are smaller, salmon egg hooks are more expensive.

Other odd hooks you might see (double curved, long shanked, or twisted) are only used in special fishing situations. They won't have a place in your tackle box for awhile, but keep any odd ones you find for your hook collection. A good collection of hooks will prepare you for whatever kind of fishing comes your way.

From time to time, your hooks will get snagged while fishing, especially if you are fishing in places where fish hide. To save a hook, first try pulling your line straight back. If this doesn't work, walk up or down the shore away from the snag and try pulling again. When fishing on a river, walk upstream. You can also pull until the line is very tight and then let go suddenly. This will sometimes pop the hook free. Do not do this with your hand line, or you will lose everything.

Never jerk the line. Always pull firmly and steadily. There will be times when you can neither pull your hook free nor wade out and retrieve it. At such times, remember how you obtained your first equipment and be pleased that you may be helping someone else get started.

Weights (Sinkers)

Lead weights allow the line to be cast—the heavier the weight the farther the cast. Weights, or sinkers, get the bait to the bottom or hold the bait at a desired level. Weights come in all shapes and sizes, figure 3-5. Despite their simple purpose, they have been designed in many different ways and for many different situations. Whatever weight you find should work.

If you are buying weights, split shot is the cheapest and has more uses. Split shot comes in many different sizes, but there are only two main types. The first is the regular old-fashioned, round type. These are easy to put on, but a problem to pry off the line. The second type clamps onto the line in the same manner, but has a forked tail in the back that, when squeezed together, opens the jaws, figure 3-5 (2,3).

The size of your weight is important. A large weight will let you cast a mile but will also sink deeper into

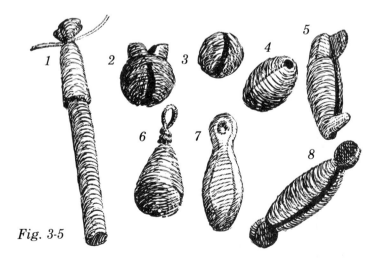

Fig. 3-5

snags. It can also prevent you from feeling the fish strike. For easier fishing, get split shot no larger than one-fourth inch across. That way if you need more weight, simply put on another split shot.

Let's take a look at the other weights that are shown in figure 3-5.

The clinch-on (5) has a groove running the length of it and lead flaps at either end. The line is placed in the groove, and the flaps are clamped over it.

The twist-on (8) has a piece of rubber down its middle. To secure the weight, lay the line on the rubber and twist the tabs at either end in opposite directions. These cigar-shaped weights have the advantage of being thin and, therefore, are less likely to snag.

Pencil sinkers (1) are also long and thin, but only one end is connected to the line, causing it to dangle. Generally, these are attached with a piece of rubber tubing. The tube is tied to the line, and the sinker is stuck inside. That way if the weight is snagged, it will come off, saving the rest of the gear from also being lost.

Sliding egg sinkers (4) are round or egg-shaped weights with a hole through the middle. The line is threaded through the hole, and the weight is left free to slide along the line. The fish can't feel the sliding weight when they are nibbling, but the angler can still feel the fish.

The dipsey (6) and bank (7) are other tie-on weights, which are easy to use and are good for bottom fishing. There are more kinds of weights, of course. If you find an

odd one, don't throw it away. You can always find a way
to use it.

Floats (Bobbers)

As the sun warms the water, underwater insects will
hatch and swim to the surface. These are the same types
of insects the fish were feeding on at the bottom. When
the insects move, the fish begin to feed at whatever depth
the insects are swimming. Fishing on the bottom at this
time would be useless. Still, a weight is needed to cast the
bait. To prevent the weight from dragging the bait to the
bottom, a float is attached to the line above the sinker.
Anything that floats will do: a stick, a piece of styro-
foam, a cork, or a thread spool. Just tie the float as far
above the bait as you want the bait to be down in the
water.

   To make a simple float, or bobber, use a wine cork or
a thread spool. Drill a hole down the middle of the cork
with a small drill bit or burn a hole with a heated ice
pick. (A thread spool is easier to work with because it
already has a hole in the middle.) Pass the fishing line
through the hole, and insert a stick to hold the float on
the line, figure 3-6.

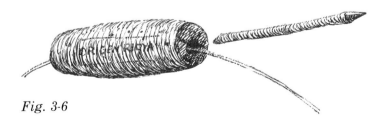

Fig. 3-6

There are times when it is hard to see the bobber way out in the water. Painting the float red and white will make it more visible. The paint will also keep wooden floats from soaking up water and sinking.

If you do not want to make a float, you can always buy one. You can also buy the popular plastic bobber. They are round and usually red and white. On one side there is a button that, when pushed, releases a wire hook on the other side. Put the line through this wire hook, and let go of the button. Now put a finger over the hook and line, and push the button again. A hook will come out of the top of the button. Put the line through this hook, and let go of the button. If you have done this correctly, the line will be attached tightly to both sides of the bobber, figure 3-7.

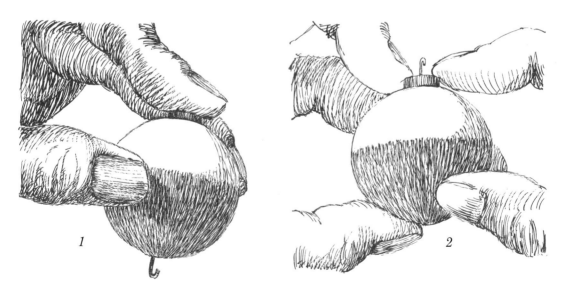

Fig. 3-7

There are times when the color of the bobber may frighten the fish, especially if you are fishing clear, shallow water. In that case you'll need to purchase clear plastic bobbers. The best size is one inch wide. Bobbers smaller than one inch can be sunk by the weight of the sinker and bait. The size is also important because a small bobber gives less resistance to a nibbling fish. With a small float it will be easier to see even the most delicate of strikes.

Stringers

What should be done with a fish once it is caught? Should it be stuffed in your pocket or down your shirt? A cold, slimy, wiggling fish inside the shirt doesn't seem exactly ideal. And a fish can't be left loose on shore, or it will flop right back into the water. A stringer is needed to solve the problem. A stringer is any device that will keep the fish from swimming away once it has been caught, and allow you to continue fishing.

Stringers are easy to make. Just cut a small, forked stick. One end should be about 2-1/2 feet long and the other about 6 inches, figure 3-8. To put a fish on the stringer, run the long part of the stick up the gills and out the mouth of the fish, figure 3-9. The short end of the

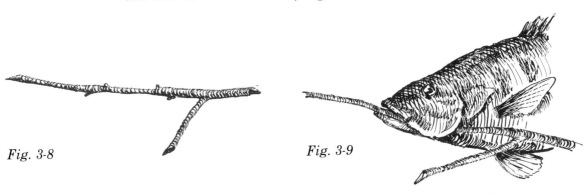

Fig. 3-8

Fig. 3-9

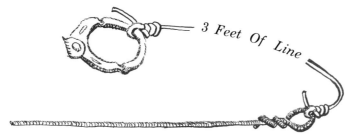

Fig. 3-10

stick will keep the fish from sliding off. As more fish are caught, slide them on top of the others. Always keep the stringer of fish in the shallow water so they will stay alive and fresh. Place a large rock on the long end of the stick so they can't swim away.

Sometime you might be fishing at a spot where a forked stick is not available. Therefore, it would be wise to have an easy-to-carry substitute. You can make a permanent stringer out of a piece of twine and a pop tab ring. If the twine is not nylon, it will need to be waxed so it will not rot. Tie the pop tab ring to one end of the twine (see Appendix: Knots) and a four- or five-inch piece of stiff wire to the other, figure 3-10.

To use the twine stringer, push the wire end through the gills and out the mouth of the fish. Then pass the wire through the pop tab ring and pull tight. For each additional fish, just slide it on as before. The first fish will keep all the others from coming off. Tie the stringer to a branch or a rock at the water's edge, and put the fish in the water.

You can buy stringers just like the ones you can make. There are also other types of stringers. They are made of wire or nylon and have a series of safety pin devices fastened to a chain. The safety pins are pushed

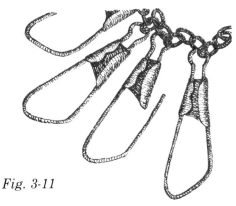

Fig. 3-11

through the lower lip of the fish and secured, figure 3-11. Each fish is put on a different safety pin.

No matter what kind of stringer you use, always place the fish in the water so they will stay alive and not spoil. Also make sure you secure the end to a solid object so the fish can't swim away—stringer and all.

Creels

Stringers are an excellent way to store your catch while fishing. If you have to travel very far to get home, however, fish, carried on a stringer, can spoil. A creel will not let that happen. A creel is just a bag or sack you keep fish in. A creel is often made from a gunnysack, which you can usually find at a livestock feed store or a grocery store. If you can't find a gunnysack, use any cloth bag, even an old pillow case. Figure 3-12 shows how the creel

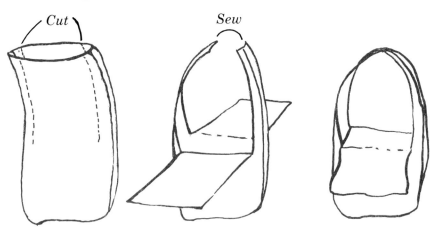

Fig. 3-12

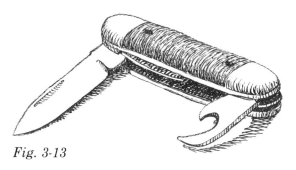

Fig. 3-13

can be made. Tie or sew the two thin ends together to form a shoulder strap, and you have a travel bag for your fish.

When you catch the first fish, wet the bag and put green grass, leaves, or ferns in the bottom. Lay the fish on the greens, and cover it with the flaps. As you catch more fish, keep layering grass and fish, grass and fish. When you are ready to leave for home, dip the creel in the water. The air will cause the water soaked up by the bag to evaporate. The layered grass and the evaporation of the water will keep the fish fresh.

You can also buy canvas or basket creels, but both are expensive. They are nice, but they work no better.

Knife

Don't forget that important and essential tool, the pocket-knife. It is useful for cutting line, opening split shot, cleaning fish, cutting a willow pole, and whittling lures. The boy or girl scout kind with two to four blades is perfect. The knife should have a main cutting blade two to three inches long and, perhaps, a smaller blade as well. A can opener or a bottle opener blade is a handy extra. Be sure to keep a pocketknife along with the rest of your fishing kit, figure 3-13.

Storing the Equipment

So far you have collected a fair amount of equipment. Now you need a place to keep it. If you don't mind having

Fig. 3-14

everything in different places, try the following. Put your hooks in the simple cardboard hook wallet described earlier, figure 1-10. If your hooks have leaders, put a rubber band around the cardboard and the leaders to hold them in place.

Your weights and bobbers can be kept in a plastic sandwich bag and stuffed in another pocket. The line can be wrapped around a smooth, fat stick or a pop can. Use a piece of tape or a rubber band to keep the line from coming undone.

You can also use a small metal bandage box to store the equipment in. Wrap the fishing line around the outside, and hold it with a piece of tape.

You could buy a small, unbreakable, plastic, tackle box. One that is 7 inches long, 3-1/2 inches wide, and 1-1/4 inches deep is perfect. You can buy one from a sporting goods store, hardware store, and even in stores with kitchen supplies.

A plastic school box also makes a dandy and inexpensive tackle box. Glue or tape a piece of cardboard on the inside of the lid to put the hooks in. Put the rest of your gear in, and write your name on the outside. Now you have a place for everything and everything is in its place, figure 3-14.

Rods and Reels

At a sporting goods or hardware store you will find graphite and split bamboo rods, as well as fiberglass. Forget the graphite and bamboo rods; it would take years of mowing lawns, baby-sitting, and collecting aluminum cans to save enough to buy those expensive rods. Instead, look at the fiberglass ones. They work just as well and look just as good as the others. The label will tell you what the rod is made of, as well as the price. Look at the five- to six-foot long rods. This length will work best for you.

In order to find out how good each rod is, perform a simple test. Hold the rod by the handle, and whip the tip up and down. A good rod will swing a great deal at the tip, but less and less closer to the handle. Avoid the rods that either are too stiff and bend like a broomstick or too flimsy and bend at the base.

Try many different rods. You will soon see and feel the difference between a good one and a bad one. Now look at the price tag of the ones that bend as they should. The color of the rod does not matter, but if it is good to look at, good to use, and the price is affordable, buy it.

Now look for a reel that fits the rod you have chosen. Many times the manufacturer will make a specific reel for a rod. It is usually best to buy a combination rod and reel—one that is made for the other. Rod and reel combinations are often offered at sale prices. These can be a good buy. Otherwise, you must buy a separate reel that will fit your rod.

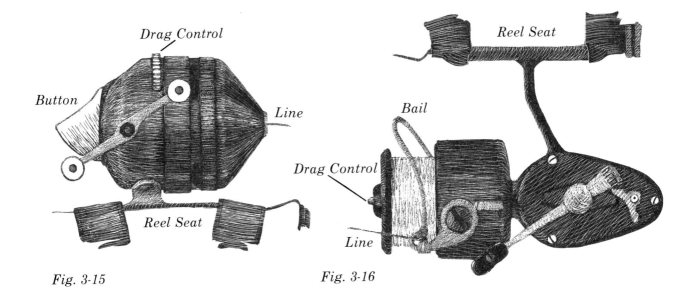

Drag Control

Button

Line

Reel Seat

Fig. 3-15

Reel Seat

Bail

Drag Control

Line

Fig. 3-16

A five- or six-foot rod does not require a very large reel. The reel should be light so it will be comfortable to cast. In any case, follow the advice of the salesperson, as long as the suggestions are within the guidelines outlined here and the amount you want to spend.

A closed-face spinning reel, figure 3-15, is the least expensive. It is fairly trouble free and easy to use. Select a major brand name like Zebco, Garcia, or Shakespeare. They have been making reels for many years and usually stand behind their products.

Open-face reels, figure 3-16, cost more but are very popular. They do not have the front portion covered as do closed-face reels so you can easily change spools of fishing line. Both reels are easy to use, but the closed-face reel is recommended for beginning anglers because it is the simplest. Reels are available for right or left hands.

Casting with a Closed-Face Reel

If you have chosen a closed-face reel, insert the reel
seat into the slot on the rod and secure it so that the
round end, where the line comes out, is facing the rod tip,
figure 3-17. Now push the button on the back of the reel.

Fig. 3-17

This will release the line. Pull the line out, and string it
through each guide on the rod. Tie a weight on the end
of the line (see Appendix: Knots), and find a nice, large,
open spot to practice casting. The reel should be on top of
the rod while you grip the handle behind it, figure 3-17.
To wind in some line, crank the reel clockwise only.

   To cast, leave six inches of line hanging from the rod
tip, and place your thumb on the release button. Extend

your arm and rod straight out behind you with the rod parallel to the ground. Push the button with your thumb, and hold the button down. Whip the rod forward, either from the side or overhand, releasing the button at the same time, figure 3-18. The weight should pull the line out in the direction you point the rod. If the line went up rather than out, you released the button too soon. If the line hit the ground in front of you, you released the button too late. Practice until you can cast the weight to any spot you aim for.

Fig. 3-18

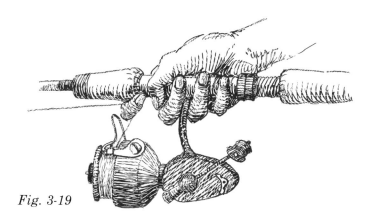

Fig. 3-19

Casting with an Open-Face Reel

Place the open-face reel on the rod with the fishing line facing the rod tip, figure 3-19. An open-face reel does not have a button to push. A bail wire keeps the line from reeling out, figure 3-16. An open-face reel hangs on the bottom of the rod and cranks counterclockwise to wind in the line. Flip the bail over to the other side to release the line. String the line through the guides of the rod, and tie a weight to the end of the line. Turn the crank and the bail will flip back automatically.

To cast, hold the rod in your hand with two fingers in front of the reel post and two fingers behind. With your index finger, hook the line and hold it against the rod, figure 3-19. Flip the bail wire from one side of the reel to the other, releasing the line so only your finger is holding it. Cast the same as with a closed-face reel, only this time release the line with your finger. As with the closed-face reel, practice until you can cast a weight wherever you would like it to go. Then you are ready to go fishing.

Using a Rod and Reel

Because of the extra wear a rod and reel put on nylon line, it is important to check and replace the line more often. When you put new line on, there are a few things you must do for trouble-free fishing.

The first thing is to tie the end of the new line to the reel spool (see Appendix: Knots). If you ever catch a record fish that pulls all your line out, you'll be very glad you did.

Next, be sure to keep the line tight as you reel it on. If you put the line on loosely, your first cast will result in a tangled mess.

Finally, fill the reel spool with line. A half-full spool will not let you cast very far. But if you fill it too full, you'll have a tangle again.

Now you have to set your drag. On the closed-face reel the drag is the dial on the side, figure 3-15, and on the open-face reel the dial is on the top, figure 3-16. By tightening or loosening these dials, you control how hard it is to pull line off the reel without turning the crank.

A well-set drag lets a fish pull the line out when it's fighting very hard. It will also hold a fish and let you reel it in when the fish tires. If the drag is set too tight, the fish will stretch and probably break the line. On the other hand, if the drag is loose, you'll never get the fish in. In either case, it's simple to adjust the drag even while you have a fish on the line.

When you hook a fish, don't start cranking the line in right away. Let the fish fight the drag awhile and tire out. Remember to keep your rod tip up so the fish fights the pole, too. When the fish is tired and you're bringing it in, be careful that you never reel in so much line that you have less than a rod's length between the tip of the rod and the fish. A shorter length of line will give the fish a chance to break loose. Once you have the fish in that far, back up and drag it on shore.

The pleasures of fishing do not require a great deal of equipment. No matter how much or how little you have, it is pleasant and natural to dream of more. Let nothing interfere with the fun of fishing and dreaming.

CHAPTER 4

Bait

The more fish Billy caught, the longer the morning grew for Dare. He hadn't caught a fish, and it seemed that his friend, who was catching them right and left, wasn't really trying. Billy just cast downstream and dipped his pole in and out of the water as he reeled in.

"Are you washing your pole or something?" Dare finally yelled.

"Yeah," Billy said with a smile, "or something."

Dare frowned and cast his worm upstream again. He concentrated especially hard on his rod tip for signs of a bite as his worm drifted downstream. Nothing happened. Billy whooped again. Dare turned his attention to his friend, who was fighting yet another fish.

"I give up. What are you doing?" Dare called to his friend.

"Washing my pole," Billy answered, smiling as Dare glared at him.

"Okay, okay!" Billy laughed. "Cast downstream and hold your pole tip deep in the water. When you reel in, raise and lower the pole so the worm will move up and down."

Dare waited until Billy was not looking before he tried the new method. He didn't have to dip his rod twice before he had a fish on his line.

The action of the bait in the water can make a big difference in the way fish react. Billy had learned to give the bait a new action that caught fish. Just using worms is not enough to assure you of good fishing. Learning lots of ways to fish with different types of bait will help you catch more fish.

Worms

Worms catch fish—probably more fish than any other single bait. Before we learn any new techniques, let's review some old ones for fishing the worm. If you are fishing still water, the worm can be fished on the bottom with a weight or off the bottom with a bobber. When bottom fishing, place the weight about twelve inches above the hook. The weight helps you cast and pulls the bait to the bottom, a favorite feeding place for fish. Alertness and a tight line will help you feel the fish biting so you can set the hook quickly.

When bobber fishing a worm, remember, the distance the float is attached above the bait determines how deep the bait will be held in the water. When deciding how deep the bait should be, you will need to answer three questions: how deep is the water, can you cast, and how deep are the fish feeding? The last question can only be answered by experimenting. Fish the worm at a variety of depths until you catch a fish. Always keep a close watch on the bobber for faint twitches, odd movement, or its complete disappearance. These are signs a fish is biting.

Whether you are bobber or bottom fishing, try a variety of locations on the water. By doing so you will soon discover where fish are feeding and have a better chance of catching something. Always keep in mind that fish sometimes change their habits, and can be downright contrary. That's what makes fishing so much of an adventure.

Casting and retrieving your worm so it is moving through the water is another method to try. This kind of worm fishing needs to be done in more open water, next to snags rather than in them. Put a worm on the hook, head first, so it covers the hook completely. Pinch off all but an inch of the worm that dangles below the hook. If the whole worm is left on, the fish might bite it off well behind the hook and get a good meal without getting caught. Attach a weight eighteen inches above the hook—the amount of weight depending on how deep you want the worm to travel as you retrieve it.

To know what causes fish to strike is difficult, and they can be very particular. If one retrieval method does not work, you must try another and then another until you find the right one. Try a slow retrieve at first, making sure you keep the worm off the bottom. Later, if that doesn't work, pull the worm faster, trying different speeds. Alternate between fast and slow speeds during the retrieve or use a jerky retrieve. Another method is the rolling retrieve. Pull in some line so the worm raises up; then let the line go slack so the worm drops. Quickly reel in the slack line and repeat these steps. The worm should be checked after each cast because this method tends to tear the worm from the hook.

To fish with worms in moving water, you'll want to rig up a little differently. Instead of putting the weight right on the line, use a small dropper line, figure 4-1. This way if the weight snags, you won't lose everything. Using a bobber in moving water is often a good idea to help keep you out of snag trouble. Cast upstream and allow the current to carry the bait down to the fish. You do this because fish lie facing upstream so they can watch for food floating down. Let the worm drift without pulling or moving the bait in any way. When the worm has drifted below you, bring it in. Many times fish will strike the worm while it is being reeled in, so stay alert. Try many different locations on the river or stream until you find the fish. If the fish are biting when you retrieve the worm and not when it is drifting, abandon the drift and cast across or downstream and reel in immediately.

Fig. 4-1

Finally, you can use worms with lures (see chapter 5). You can put a worm on the hook of a spinner or plug. Both the movement of the worm and the smell will help attract a fish. A short one-half-inch section of a worm on a wet fly hook can also catch more fish.

We have already covered the ways to gather worms in chapter 1, but if you become an angler who likes to fish with worms, you might want to raise these little fellows. This is a simple task and one that is much less of a chore than raising rabbits!

To begin, you'll need a place to keep your worms. A

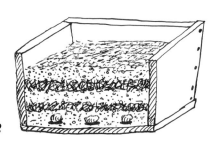

Fig. 4-2

large wooden box works best. A box three feet long, two feet wide, and two feet deep would provide plenty of room, figure 4-2. If you do not want to make your own wooden box, two or three wooden fruit crates will work well. You can save space by stacking them one on top of the other. If you live in an apartment, maybe you could use a window planter box or a very large flower pot.

Holes should be drilled in the bottom of the box so water can drain out. To keep the worms from crawling out, place a stone over each hole. The water can still drain, but the worms will stay in. If you are using fruit crates, put newspaper in the bottom to cover the cracks.

Dig up loose dirt, and gather some dead leaves or grass cuttings to fill the box. You will also need some garbage. Put a thick layer of leaves or grass cuttings on the bottom over the rocks or newspaper. Add a thick layer of dirt, and wet the soil. The box should be over half full of dirt and leaves at this point. Dump in your garbage and some more leaves. The garbage can be leftover food, coffee grounds, and any other material that tends to rot quickly. Make sure you do not gather more garbage than your box can hold; otherwise your neighbors will complain, and cats will gather. Two one-pound coffee cans, full of kitchen scraps, will do nicely. Chop the garbage into small bits, and bury some in the dirt in the box. Dump the remaining garbage on top. Cover the garbage with more leaves and dirt, filling the box nearly to the brim.

Give the soil a good wetting but not so much that it's

muddy—just enough so it's evenly damp from top to bottom. The soil must be kept damp with a light sprinkling every other day. Continue to add more garbage every other week to keep the soil rich and the worms fed. The amount of garbage depends on the size of your box. A one-pound coffee can of garbage added once a month will be about right for a large box or three fruit crates.

Try to keep the box in the shade. A lid will help to keep things cool. If the box gets too hot or the dirt dries out, the worms will die. Above all, keep the soil damp.

Unless you find worms when digging for dirt, you will have to find or buy some live ones to stock your farm. The worms will multiply and become fatter and larger, providing you with all the bait you'll ever need. If your worm farm is big enough, you may find you have more worms than you'll need. You can sell your extra worms to local anglers and begin saving money for that new fishing rod.

Grasshoppers

In the heat of summer, insects are plentiful, and fish love to eat them. For this reason insects make great bait. This is especially true with grasshoppers. Although grasshoppers are great jumpers and fliers, they are not very careful to watch where they are going and will often land in the water. When they do, fish smile and race each other to see which one gets to eat the poor, floundering hopper. To a fish, the hopper is a triple dip ice cream cone, which they can't resist.

Early morning is the best time to catch grasshoppers.

The best time to gather grasshoppers is early in the morning. The cool night air slows the hoppers' activity, and they are easy to grab. You will find them clinging to almost anything that is low to the ground. Gather and keep them in a covered container. Punch holes in the lid so your hoppers will stay alive. Cram in as many as possible. When the fishing is good, you'll need them all. If you wait until the warmer part of the day, catching them will not be so easy. They will hop and fly out of reach just as you think you have them.

Grasshopper activity does not go unnoticed by the fish. They wake up plenty early to get ready for the feast, so morning is the time to be on the water. Make sure your hooked grasshopper is the first one the fish sees. Remember, however, although the morning is a good time to use hoppers for bait, the fish will feed on them all day.

To fish the hopper in still water, you'll need a hook, bobber, and split shot. If you want to fish the hopper on the surface of the water, leave off the split shot. You should use a clear bobber. The fish will be looking up for the hopper, and you don't want anything floating by to scare the fish. There are two ways to put the grasshopper on the hook. Either stick the hook into its mouth and back through the body and out the belly, or hook the hopper through the segment behind the head, figure 4-3.

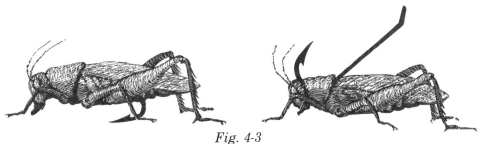

Fig. 4-3

Before fishing, check the water to see if any fish are rising to eat hoppers. If you don't see any activity, choose your own spot. If a fish does not strike very soon, and your hopper isn't moving, give the line a little twitch so the grasshopper looks like it is struggling.

If you have no luck fishing the hopper on top of the water, put a split shot on the line between the bait and the bobber and cast out again. You can even take the bobber off and fish the hopper on the bottom. Sometimes, even when you can see a fish rising, the fish will wait until the hopper sinks before eating it.

When you fish a hopper on top of moving water, rig the hook and bobber the same as you did when fishing still water. Cast the hopper upstream from any fish you see rising, and let the bait drift downstream. Never let your line hold or drag the hopper while it is drifting. The hopper should drift naturally with the current. If it does not, the fish will see that something is wrong and not strike.

Grasshoppers are often pulled under by the current in moving water. Fish hiding around eddies, fast water, and on bends in the stream count on this to happen. They stay near the bottom, waiting for the hoppers to come to them. Go after these fat, lazy fish by adding a small split shot to your line. If the water is deep, take the bobber off and cast upstream from one of these areas, and let the hopper drift down. The split shot will pull the grasshopper underwater where the fish are hungrily waiting.

Crickets

Crickets are very much like grasshoppers except they live in different places and sing songs at night. You'll find crickets under rocks, logs, trash, or anything else that they can hide under. Although they are a little softer than grasshoppers, they can be hooked and are fished the same way, figure 4-4. If you don't use all your crickets while fishing and want to save them for the next trip, keep them in a warm container with plenty of holes in the lid. Give crickets something juicy to eat, like a piece of apple, potato, or celery, and they can live up to a month.

Caterpillars

Caterpillars make good bait as long as you stay away from the fuzzy ones. Hairy caterpillars are poisonous. You don't have to worry about handling them—just don't eat one. Fish know better than to eat poisonous caterpillars. Caterpillars are put on the hook and fished the same as worms, figure 4-5.

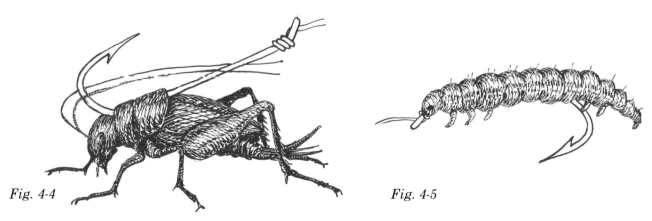

Fig. 4-4   *Fig. 4-5*

Beetles

Small beetles can make good bait, too. They are very hard, stay on the hook well, and fish love to eat them. You can find beetles under rocks, boards, and around the edges of your house. Hook them through the hard plate in front of their wings, and fish them like a grasshopper, figure 4-6.

Hellgrammites

Fish also feed on insects that live in the water. One of these is the hellgrammite. By turning over a rock, you may find one clinging to it or trying to swim away. Be quick and grab the insect, and you've caught yet another tasty delight for the fish.

Hellgrammites are hooked just like a hopper, and you fish them like a worm, figure 4-7. There are other underwater insects big enough to stick on a hook. Just turn over rocks and logs in the water, search through water weeds, and root around in the mud. When fishing is slow, hunting for insects is a good way to occupy your time.

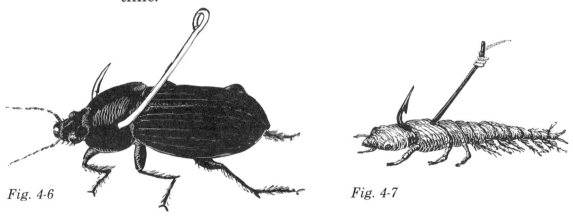

Fig. 4-6   Fig. 4-7

Hellgrammites can be found under rocks and make excellent fish bait.

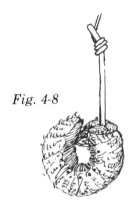
Fig. 4-8

Grubs

You may find grubs when digging for worms. Grubs are wormlike larvae of insects. Keep them as they make excellent bait. Because a grub is soft, make sure the hook is pierced through its hard head as well as its body, figure 4-8.

Fig. 4-9

Mealworms

These tough little grubs catch fish and are easy to raise. Buy one can of them, and you'll never need to buy another. Find a large, empty can, at least two gallon, and fill it three-fourth full with cornmeal, flour, and sawdust. Drop in the mealworms, and put on a lid punched full of tiny holes. Soon you will see beetles running around inside. Don't throw them out because they will make more mealworms. Hook and fish mealworms just like earthworms, figure 4-9.

Other Insects

Fish will also occasionally feed on cockroaches, dragonflies, butterflies, moths, bees, horseflies, maggots, and many other insects that fall on the water. These insects are fished the same as hoppers, but you will find them more difficult to catch.

Those insects that are too small to put on a hook, like mosquitoes and mayflies, are also favorite fish foods. To take advantage of this, anglers have invented ways to imitate these tiny insects. The result is called fly fishing. We'll tell you more about that in the next chapter.

Snails

If while searching about in the water for bait you run across some water snails, pick them up. These snails, or periwinkles as some call them, make good bait. Smash the shell, and remove the meat. Thread the meat on the hook and bottom fish the snail, figure 4-10.

Fig. 4-10

What type of insect you choose to fish with should be determined by watching the water to see what insects the fish are feeding on. If you don't know, take different kinds of baits along to cover all the possibilities.

Minnows

Have you ever noticed schools of minnows darting wildly about and jumping out of the water? Well, those little fish were trying to escape from a big fish that wanted to eat them. That is why minnows make such fine bait. The type and size of minnow that you use depends on the type of fish you hope to catch. For example, crappie and trout are caught only on small minnows. Northern pike, on the other hand, are caught on much larger minnows. Check with your local bait store to find out the type and size minnows that are best for your specific fishing needs.

When fishing live minnows, there are three ways to put them on a hook. The hook can be placed in the back under the dorsal fin, just in front of the tail, or through both lips, figure 4-11. In each case a short hook is best—like the salmon egg hooks. These hooks will be less visible and do less damage to the minnow.

Whether you are fishing still or moving water, the minnow can be fished without a bobber or split shot. This way the minnow is freely swimming around, attracting fish. Cast the minnow upstream in moving water, and, except for taking in slack, let the minnow swim freely until a fish strikes. If you want the minnow to swim near or at the bottom, put a split shot on above the minnow. If you would like to know when a fish is playing with the bait, put a bobber on well above the minnow. Then if a fish strikes, you will be able to see the bobber go underwater. Remember that a live minnow will move the bobber around, so don't try to set the hook until the bobber goes under.

If you use dead minnows, you can fish them whole or cut up. To fish dead minnows whole, hook them the same as a live minnow. Since they are dead, you must give them the appearance of being alive. Large fish are generally lazy and prefer eating injured or ill minnows. The action that you want to achieve is one that makes the minnow look poorly. Cast the minnow out, reel in a couple of feet, and stop for a second. Keep repeating this method so the minnow will move like an injured fish—

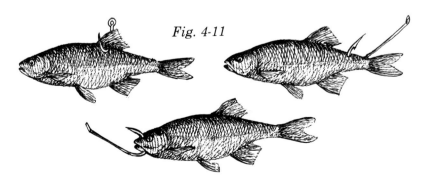

Fig. 4-11

swimming, then floating, then swimming again. In moving water all you have to do is jerk the line slightly every once in a while because the water will also make the dead minnow move. Another way to use a dead minnow is still fishing on the bottom or under a bobber, like fishing a worm. A cut up minnow is put on a hook to cover it and is fished the same as a worm.

When you are using frozen minnows, do not let them thaw completely. If they do, the minnow will get so soft that it falls off the hook. Keep them frozen until you put them on the hook.

Fig. 4-12

It is fun to catch minnows; after all, that is fishing, too. Minnows are fairly easy to catch. All you need is a net—one with tiny holes like a screen. You can easily make a net from an old pair of pantyhose. Tie the legs in a knot, open a wire coat hanger, and bend the wire to form a circle. Sew the open end of the pantyhose around the coat hanger, figure 4-12. If you don't have an old pair of pantyhose, use a piece of cheese cloth. Fold a piece in half, sew two sides together, and sew the open end onto a coat hanger.

With the new net in hand, it's time to fish for minnows. Go to the nearest lake or pond, and walk along the edge, or walk out on a pier. Look for large groups, or schools, of minnows. When you spot them, put the net in the water. The net will frighten the minnows away at first. But if you leave it very still, they should return. When a couple of minnows swim near, scoop them up and put them in a bucket of lake water to keep them alive.

Catching minnows is as much fun as fishing with them.

If you find the minnows unwilling to come close to the net, try coaxing them. Pinch off bits of bread and toss them in the water near the net. With practice, you will seldom miss catching at least a few minnows.

Another fun method of catching minnows is to use a tiny hook, a short piece of line, and bread for bait. It's just like fishing for big fish only you get to watch all the action from a nose distance away. Minnows do not live very long in a bucket, so use them the same day you catch them. To lengthen their life, scoop out a cup of water and dribble it back in the bucket so it bubbles up. By doing this, you are adding more oxygen, which allows the minnows to live much longer.

In some states it is against the law to fish with live minnows. This law is to prevent minnows from breeding in waters where they are unwanted. Certain types of minnows are trash fish. Trash fish are fish that are generally considered poor eating, and people do not like to catch and keep them. Because they are not bothered by anglers, trash fish increase rapidly, compared to the more popular fish. The trash fish begin to outfeed, outnumber, and soon replace other fish. Check the fish and game regulations in your state before using live minnows. If the state forbids their use, or you are not interested in introducing a trash fish into a favorite fishing hole, freeze the minnows and use them dead.

If you catch a trash fish, don't throw it back into the water. Keep the unwanted fish for bait. Large trash fish can be cut up and used to catch certain bottom-feeding fish, like the catfish. Even the guts are good bait. Certain bottom feeders find their food by smell, so the smellier the bait the better. Put a stinky glob on the hook and cast into a deep, dark hole. Be prepared because a hungry, whiskered catfish can grow mighty big.

Crayfish

Whenever a fish feels like having a fancy dinner, it will eat crayfish. Crayfish are good to eat and, therefore, make great bait. They are a lot of fun to catch, too, if you watch your fingers.

You will see crayfish coming out of little holes in muddy ditches, in small ponds, and in shallow areas of lakes. There are different ways to catch crayfish; try them all and see which works for you.

You should know a few things about crayfish that will make catching them easier. First, the crayfish always swims backwards, using its tail to move through the water. Second, its eyes are up on stalks so the crayfish can see all around and is, therefore, hard to sneak up on. Fortunately, the third thing about crayfish is that it points its antennae in the direction it is looking.

In streams and creeks shallow enough to wade in, find an area where you have spotted crayfish or where the bottom is rocky. Place a friend with a net downstream from you, and start stirring up the bottom with a stick. With all this fuss going on, the crayfish will be driven from their hiding places and drift with the current down to the person with the net.

You can also catch crayfish with a length of string and a strip of raw bacon. Roll the bacon up and tie it securely in a compact lump to the end of the string. Set a net flat on the bottom of the pond, just in front of you. Toss the bacon out into the water, and let a crayfish get hold of it. Slowly pull the string toward you. Crayfish are especially greedy and will hang on as long as you don't pull too fast or drag them out of the water. When the crayfish is over the net, scoop it up. If you have no net, hold your hand in the water and grab the crayfish from behind.

Store the crayfish in a bucket of water or a clean, plastic bleach bottle with a hand size hole cut in the top. To hold a crayfish, grab it by the sides so it won't pinch you, figure 4-13. Before you put the crayfish in the bucket, grab each pincer and bend it sharply backwards, breaking it off. This will not hurt the crayfish, but it will keep the crayfish from hurting you or each other. Crayfish are terrible fighters when placed in a bucket together. Don't let them get hot or dried out unless you are trying to make a rotten bunch of stink bait.

A hook on the end of your line is all that is needed to fish the crayfish. Put the hook into the tail, and your bait will remain alive and active, attracting lots of fish, figure 4-14. Don't put the hook through the blue line running

Fig. 4-13

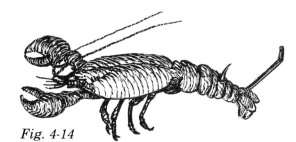

Fig. 4-14

down the tail, or it will kill the bait. Cast the crayfish out into the water, and let it crawl around, doing whatever it wants to. When you feel the crayfish stop moving, that means it has found a place to hide. Give the line a tug to pull the crayfish out in the open and back on the job. As long as it is crawling around, the crayfish is inviting a fish to supper.

You can also use the crayfish for bait when it is cut into pieces. Put a piece on a hook with split shot to fish the bottom, or use a bobber and fish closer to the surface. All dead bait is fished like a worm, both in still and moving water.

Frogs

Frogs are a good bait if you find them where you are fishing. A net is a helpful tool to have while hunting frogs. Frogs are quick and usually only give you one shot at catching them. Search for them in wet meadows and in the thick grass around the edge of your fishing hole. You will also see them in the water with their head and eyes just sticking out or sitting on something in the water. Be fast with the net, placing it well out in front of the frog (in case it jumps as you are swinging the net). Grab a frog with your hands if you have to. Don't worry, it won't give you warts!

When you fish with a frog for bait, use only a hook at the end of the line. The hook size should match the size of the frog—a large hook for a large frog and a small hook for a small frog. Hook the frog through both lips and cast it out, figure 4-15. The frog will swim around fighting the hook and line, which makes this bait very attractive to the fish.

Other Live Baits

There are other live baits which anglers sometimes use. These baits can include salamanders, shrimp, mullet, crabs, small snakes, lizards, mussels, clams, leeches, mice, and on and on. Check with your local fish and game department for more information about unique baits used in your area.

Fish Eggs, Fish Eyes, and Domestic Baits

Fish eggs or salmon eggs are good trout bait but will work for other fish, also. Salmon eggs can be bought in sporting goods stores, although they are expensive. If you buy salmon eggs, you will also need the short salmon egg hooks, figure 3-4. To bait the salmon egg, put the hook through the egg close to one edge, and slide it up the shank. Now turn the egg around, and lower it onto the point of the hook so it is completely covered, figure 4-16.

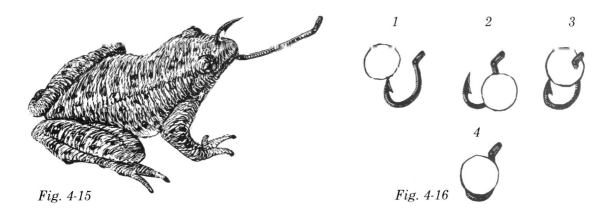

Fig. 4-15

Fig. 4-16

Fish the salmon eggs in still or moving water just like you would a worm.

You can avoid buying salmon eggs by making your own fish egg bait. Have you ever noticed a yellow, white, or orange pair of roe clusters in a fish while cleaning it? What you saw were fish eggs. Next time you find them—save them. When you get home, spread some newspaper on the table and put a handful of borax (cleaning powder) on the paper. Cut the egg clusters into whatever size pieces you want, and drop them into the pile of borax. Put another handful of borax into a paper bag, and put all the pieces of egg cluster inside. Close the top of the bag, and shake the contents until all the clusters are covered with borax. Next, pour out the egg clusters onto the pile of borax on the newspaper. Fold the paper up around the eggs, and tie it with a string so it will not come open. Put the package in the refrigerator for two or three days. The eggs can also be stored in a sealed plastic bag. Keep the eggs refrigerated until you want to use them. Hook and fish this type of bait just like a single salmon egg.

Fish eyes are a good bait to use to catch those whopper fish. After you have caught a fish with a worm, pluck out an eye with your knife and fish it like a salmon egg. There could be a whopper fish in it for you.

Another type of fish bait that is easy to find is the domestic variety. This bait can include marshmallows, cheese balls, corn kernels, and who knows what else. The very same things you buy at the grocery store and eat, you can also use for bait. Take care that you don't try both eating and baiting at the same time. You might end up eating a worm or a grasshopper!

Make sure that the domestic bait hides the hook. Salmon egg hooks work well when only one item is being used. Larger hooks may require two or three marshmallows or corn kernels to cover them. Most of the baits of this type will stay on the hook, but cheese can be a bit of a problem. To prevent losing cheese bait, use soft cheese mixed with some cotton and rolled into little balls. The cotton will help keep the cheese together and on the hook.

Fish these domestic baits just like a salmon egg or a worm. Although they are useful in all kinds of water and in many situations, the fish that seem to like domestic bait the best are the planters, or stocked fish. Planters are fish that are raised in a fish hatchery and released into rivers and lakes to replace fish that have been caught.

Many people like to prepare their own baits like a chef creates a new recipe. Usually these are a variety of dough balls consisting of cornmeal flour or wheat flour mixed with other ingredients. The other ingredients are thrown in for flavor or smell. Chopped liver is one of those delightful ingredients! Mix the flour with water to make a dough, and roll the chopped liver inside it. You can also roll up small pieces of bread with chopped liver.

Dough balls are pressed onto the hook, usually treble hooks, and fished like a salmon egg. Using such unusual baits will catch something, don't you think?

Certainly all the baits ever used by anglers have not been covered. What you know now, however, should take care of the majority of fish and fishing situations. The next chapter will introduce you to a whole new class of fish catchers called lures.

CHAPTER 5
Artificial Lures

Why would anyone be interested in catching fish with something artificial? There is more than enough live bait to keep anglers happy and busy catching fish for years. Well, there are more reasons than you might think. To fool a fish into striking feathers, yarn, wood, plastic, or flashy metal requires greater skill while it adds an exciting and new adventure to fishing. Besides, you will have the added thrill of catching a fish with something you invented and made yourself. Through your skill alone, the fish will eat something that can't be eaten. An artificial lure, therefore, can be used over and over again. It won't die, and it certainly can't stink up the refrigerator.

Most artificial lures are made to resemble the food fish eat. Others are fancy inventions, pieced together from the tatter of an angler's fine dreams and look more like baby martians than minnows. But that doesn't matter. What does matter is they catch fish.

Spoons
One artificial lure is the spoon, which probably became a lure by accident. Imagine an angler out of luck and bait, sitting in his boat on a hot afternoon, idly spooning

Fig. 5-1

cottage cheese into his mouth. By accident, he drops his spoon overboard. He watches as the spoon flashes its way to the bottom. Suddenly, a fish spies the shiny object and, thinking it is something to eat, gobbles it up. The angler smiles to himself. A new idea for a lure has been discovered. Today there is an unbelievable range of sizes, weights, metals, and colors of spoons to choose from.

When one sees the action or movement the spoon makes as it is pulled through the water, it is easy to understand why the spoon is a successful lure. It looks like a minnow flashing and darting about. The shape of the spoon determines its action. The weight of the spoon determines how far it can be cast and how deep the lure will run in the water.

Fig. 5-2

Although fishing spoons no longer resemble table spoons, they have kept the cup shape, figure 5-1. At each end holes are drilled. In one hole a hook is attached with a small split ring and to the other the fishing line is tied. Use a snap swivel to attach the spoon to the line. The spoon alone wobbles and turns so much that it twists the line. A twisted line becomes tangled easily, and tangled line is an enemy of the angler. The snap swivel consists of a loop at one end to tie the line to and a safety pin snap at the other to hold the spoon. In the middle is the swivel that turns with the spoon to keep the line from twisting, figure 5-2. The snap swivel is a necessary device for lure anglers.

To fish the spoon in still water, snap it to your line

with a swivel and cast out your line. When the lure hits the water, begin to retrieve immediately. The retrieve moves the spoon through the water and creates the action. Try a variety of retrieves, just like fishing a worm. Use a steady, fast, or slow retrieve or a jerky one, imitating an injured minnow. An alternating slow, then fast, retrieve can make the spoon look like a scared minnow and will excite larger fish.

Use the spoon at a variety of depths. When you cast the spoon, wait a few seconds before starting to retrieve. Count as you wait. If you catch a fish at the level of a five count, you can cast and count to five again and fish the same depth.

Moving water is fished in a similar manner. The spoon needs to be kept moving, or it will be swept into a snag. Use the same retrieves as in still water fishing. Remember to avoid casting the spoon to the exact place you think a fish might be. The splash may frighten it. Instead, cast upstream a little, and let the spoon drift down to the fish.

Fishing spoons are available in any of a number of colors and metals. Find out which one works in your area by asking the local sporting goods dealers or the fish and game officer. All fishing, however, comes down to this: if the lure you are using, or the depth you are fishing, or the retrieve method you are using is not catching fish, keep changing until you find the combination that catches fish.

You may have found a spoon while hunting the

shores for other fishing gear. You can always buy fishing spoons, but why do that when you can make them. To make your own, you will only need a teaspoon. You don't need real silver unless you want to brag that your fish are all caught with silver spoons in their mouths!

Once you have a spoon, cut or break off the handle and drill a small hole at each end, figure 5-3. Wire a size 6

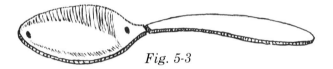

Fig. 5-3

hook to one end of the spoon with 22 gauge galvanized wire. Cut a three-fourth-inch piece and bend it in half. Stick the wire through one hole in the spoon, and slip the hook on the wire, also. Cross the two ends of the wire and, using a pair of pliers, twist the ends at least two times around, figure 5-4. You may have to hold the spoon with another pair of pliers while you twist, but don't wire the hook up too snugly. A tightly attached hook will limit the action of the spoon. The hook needs to dangle. Cut off the extra wire. Attach a snap swivel to the other hole, figure 5-5.

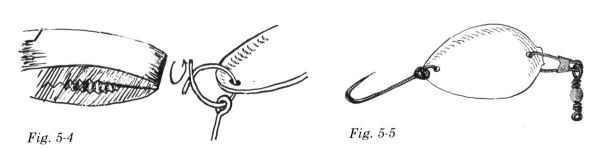

Fig. 5-4

Fig. 5-5

Paint the spoon if you want a colored lure. Be sure to use an acrylic or other waterproof paint. The color should be one that is used in your area, unless you want to experiment on your own. Otherwise, look at and copy the ones sold in the stores.

You can also change the action of the spoon by changing the shape of the lure. There are several ways of doing this. You can use a hammer to pound one end of the spoon flat, or, by using a vise, you can twist the spoon a little with a pair of pliers. You can also squeeze the ends of the spoon together so it has a deeper cup. Try making one of each kind, and you will be ready for whatever the situation demands.

You can also make fishing spoons from tabs off of pop cans. Break the ring off, and use a hammer and nail to punch a small hole at each end. Punch the hole through one side, turn it over, and punch back through the other side. The hole will have a ragged edge. Hit the hole with the hammer to flatten it. Next wire a hook to the wide end of the tab like you did for the teaspoon. Attach a small snap swivel to the narrow end, and you have a spoon, figure 5-6.

Fig. 5-6

The pop tab spoon will be very light and difficult to cast unless you add a couple of split shot to the line. Pop tab spoons can also be changed by pounding them with a hammer. You can also paint, bend, twist, or leave them alone. These little spoons are fun to use because they catch fish so readily. Put a worm on the hook, and you double the chances of getting a heavy strike.

Fig. 5-7

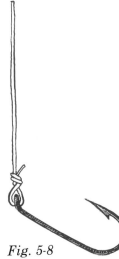

Fig. 5-8

Spinners

Another kind of lure that catches fish is the spinner. A spinner is similar to a spoon, but it has a different action. It spins around instead of wobbling and darting. Spinners are usually made from a straight wire with a hook at one end and beads and a blade along its length, figure 5-7. The blade spins around and around while the lure is being pulled through the water. Changing the retrieve method changes the action of the spinner. Spinners are fished the same as spoons but often catch fish when a spoon will not.

You can buy spinners, or you may have found one, but making your own can be fun. Find a two-inch piece of thin but stiff wire, the same 22 gauge wire used for making spoons is perfect. Gather several pop tabs and some beads. The beads can be round or oval and any color. Small beads work better, but make sure the hole in the bead is large enough to slide on the wire. Your mom may already have some beads you can use, or perhaps you can find an old necklace to take beads from. Check with your mom first.

Begin by bending the wire one-half inch from the end and slipping a size 8 hook onto the wire. Cross the two ends of the wire. Grab the crossed wires with a pair of pliers, twisting the wire around at least twice, figure 5-8. Hold the loop and hook with needle nose pliers while you twist. Cut off the short wire that sticks out beyond the twist. Slide three round beads or one oblong bead down the wire so they are above the hook. Break a pop tab from its ring, and punch a hole in the narrow end. Slip the pop tab on the wire above the beads. Make sure the hole is large enough so the blade will spin easily. Make a loop on the end of the wire one-fourth inch above the blade. To do this, wrap the wire around a nail and twist it with pliers at least twice around, figure 5-9. Now pull out the nail, cut off the extra wire, attach a snap swivel to the loop, and go fishing.

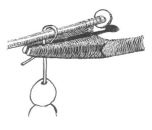

Fig. 5-9

The spinner can be changed to make it more attractive to the fish. You can use different colored beads, and the blade can be painted in a variety of colors. You can also make a multibladed spinner. Attach a hook to a three-inch wire, adding two beads and a blade. Then add two more beads and another blade on top, figure 5-10. Make the loop above the second blade, and you are finished. Treble hooks work well on both spoons and spinners but are not allowed in some states. Check the fishing regulations before using them. Add split shot to the line to give the spinner more weight for casting. Again, a worm on the hook of a spinner is an addition fish find most attractive.

Fig. 5-10

Test the lures to see that they spin or wobble properly. Take them to a place where the water is clear—the bathtub, for example, and pull them quickly through the water on the end of a short piece of line. Watch them carefully so you get a good idea of their action. If they do not sink, add a split shot. It is necessary to see their action while they are underwater. If the spinner blade doesn't spin, bend it a little. How you bend the blade depends on your individual lure—either bend it out more or flatten it.

If you have only two snap swivels, a pop tab, and a hook, you can make a very simple but useful spinner. Snap the two swivels together, and slip a hook on the bottom snap. Punch a hole in the pop tab at the narrow end, and slip it on the top snap swivel, figure 5-11. Tie your fishing line to the loop in the top swivel, and you are ready to fish. This spinner works well in emergencies. You can put one together in seconds and be fishing while others are going home for their gear.

Fig. 5-11

Plugs

Plugs are another form of artificial lure. They are pieces of wood, carved and painted to look like the food fish eat, such as frogs, minnows, and crayfish. There are thousands of different plugs on the market. Fortunately, they fall into one of three major categories: floating plugs, floating-diving plugs, and deep diving plugs.

Floating plugs are made to imitate things that swim on or near the surface of the water such as frogs, ducklings, mice, and dying minnows. Though the color and plug shape are important to fool a fish, the action of the plug is most important. To imitate a dying minnow, let the plug lay on the surface and give it a slight jerk once in awhile. A frog plug should appear to be swimming so give it short jerks. Surface plugs are best fished in shallow water and very near weeds or other objects in the water.

Floating-diving plugs imitate minnows, and nearly all have a "lip." The lip makes the plug dive and wiggle so it appears lifelike. A slow retrieve will cause the plug to dive shallow and wobble slowly like a calm, unsuspecting fish. A fast retrieve will cause the plug to dive deeper and wobble more as a scared minnow would. Vary your retrieve, and try as many retrieves as are necessary to catch fish.

The third category of plugs, deep diving, imitates those things that live at or near the bottom, such as minnows and crayfish. To make the lure dive to the bottom, a very large lip is used. Deep diving minnow plugs are best used in very deep water while being pulled behind a boat. They can be fished from shore or a pier if the water is deep. Don't let them hit the bottom. It wouldn't look natural for a minnow to be banging its head against the bottom. On the other hand, deep diving crayfish plugs should be fished bouncing along the bottom because crayfish swim on the bottom. With both plugs, cast and retrieve in as many different ways as you would a spinner or spoon.

Plugs are very expensive, so you might want to try making your own. You'll need a few simple tools and materials. A sharp pocket knife is necessary for whittling. You'll need wood to whittle on; pine, fir, and redwood are nice soft woods to use. Do not use green wood because it splits when drying. One-half-dozen small, stainless steel eye screws, one-fourth inch long, are next on the list. You'll also need a pair of needle nose pliers, a

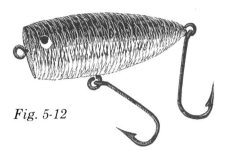

Fig. 5-12

tube of model airplane glue, and size 6 or 8 hooks. Treble hooks work best, but large, single hooks will do just fine. Last of all you will need acrylic paint.

Your floating plug will be shaped like a cigar with the flat face for popping on the surface like a swimming frog, figure 5-12. Carve the plug from the last 2-1/2 to 3 inches of a foot-long stick so you have something to hold onto while working. Make the plug round and narrowed off on the end. Don't worry if the carving does not come out perfectly. You don't even have to sand down the whittling marks. What is important is that the plug resembles the real thing, and you made it!

Once the shape is carved, cut it off the stick and drop it into a sinkful of water. Mark the side of the plug that floats under the surface as the bottom. Take two eye screws and pry open the loops with needle nose pliers. You'll be putting hooks on these later. Screw one open eye screw into the bottom of the plug, right in the middle. Place the other eye screw at the tip of the plug's narrowed end. Finally, screw a closed eye screw into the middle of the flat face for the fishing line, figure 5-12.

Paint the plug to look like a frog—dark green on top, lighter green down the sides, and yellow on the bottom. Paint a few yellow spots on the back and a black dot on each side of the front for eyes. Paint a red mouth on the flat face. Hang onto the eye screws as you paint. When

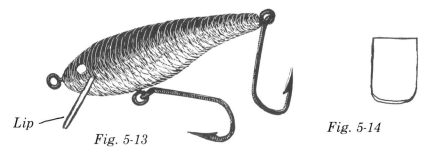

Lip

Fig. 5-13

Fig. 5-14

the paint is thoroughly dry, put the hooks on the eye screws and pinch the loops closed. If the hook eye does not fit on the eye screw, wire it on.

To make a floating-diving plug, carve a more narrow 2-1/2- to 3-inch minnowlike shape without the flat end, figure 5-13. To make the plug dive, attach a lip to it. A wood chip, 1/8 inch thick and 1 inch long and at least as wide as the plug, will make a nice lip. Cut one end square and the other round, figure 5-14. Then cut or saw a notch on the bottom of the plug. Make the notch similar in position and angle to the drawing in figure 5-13. Cut the notch slightly narrower than the lip so the lip fits in tightly. Glue the lip into the notch with waterproof glue, making sure it is in straight and even.

Attach the eye screws as you would to a floating plug. For a minnow plug, paint the top, black, the sides, dark green to light green, and the bottom, white. If you can blend the bands of color, all the better. Paint the back of the lip, white, and the front, red.

The deep diving crayfish plug is made the same as the other plugs except it has a fatter body and a longer metal lip, made from a tin can. Use tin snips to cut the lip. It should be at least 1-1/2 inches long and as wide or wider than the plug, figure 5-15. Cut a notch 1/2 inch deep, straight into the nose of the plug, making a thin slot so the lip will fit tightly. With glue on the lip, insert the lip into the notch. Drill a small hole down through the body into the lip, and pound a small finishing nail into the hole

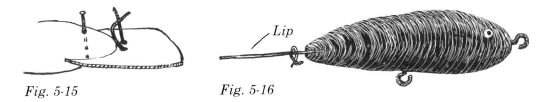

Fig. 5-15

Fig. 5-16

to help hold the lip in place, figure 5-15. Cut or file off any
of the nail that sticks out of the plug. Everything should
be glued into place to make the plug strong.

Drill or pound two holes in the center of the lip close
to the plug and insert a wire, twisting it to form a loop for
tying on the fishing line, figure 5-15. The open eye screws
are screwed in on the middle bottom and the back end for
the hooks, figure 5-16.

Paint the plug yellow-orange or red so it will show up
in deep, dark waters. As a crayfish plug, it should have
red or black stripes across the top and black eyes at the
rear. Remember, the crayfish swims backwards. If you
wish you can get fancy and drill holes in the sides and
glue rubber band legs in them.

Once the paint is dry, put the hooks on the open eye
screws and squeeze the loops shut. If you are using single
hooks, the one on the bottom should face front, and the
hook on the end should face back, figure 5-17.

For information about what plugs are used in your
area, look at the ones in the stores and notice the variety
of their shapes and colors.

Test the finished plugs to see if they work. The floating plugs should be okay, but the ones with lips may
need some adjustment. Pull the plug through the water;
if the plug flips on its back or spins, the lip is too long.
Shave or cut the lip and test it again. If the plug rides on

Fig. 5-17

one side, the lip should be shaved off on the side that rides down. When you finally have the plug diving straight, you can repaint the lip if it's made of wood.

You might wonder whether fishing with plugs doesn't catch everything within easy range, considering all the hooks that dangle off some of them. Dare and Billy were once fishing with plugs from a boat. They were anchored in fairly deep water. The wind blew the boat in a gentle circle as they cast and retrieved. Their luck was down—not a single bite. To change their luck, they decided to use deep diving plugs. Dare put on a minnow lure while Billy put on his "killer" crayfish plug.

Dare was casting off one side of the boat, and Billy worked the other. Suddenly, Billy rockd the boat as he jumped to set his hook. Not a moment later, Dare was tangling with a fish of his own. As each boy played his fish, they teased each other about who had the biggest fish on their line.

Neither boy had seen his fish. Holding their lines tight, they peered over the side, hoping to catch sight of the monsters. They continued tugging to bring them to the surface, but neither boy could budge his fish another inch. Suddenly, the sound of scratching on the bottom of the boat told the story. Dare and Billy had hooked each other's plug. The boat, as it turned in the wind, had caused their lines to become entangled. Now the lines were locked together on the bottom side of the boat. Needless to say, this experience was one fishing story neither boy bragged about.

Fig. 5-18

Jigs

Jigs are another good substitute for live minnows, figure 5-18. Use them with a cane pole, dropping the jig straight into the water and bobbing it up and down. This action is called jigging and works well for catching crappie. The jig can also be fished like a spinner with other gear.

You can make a jig by pinching a split shot on a size 4 or 6 bait hook, next to the eye. Paint the split shot white, yellow, or red, with a black dot on each side for an eye. Now get a six-inch piece of yarn, the same color as the head, to make the body and tail. Lay the yarn on the shank with, at least, an inch extending beyond the bend, figure 5-19. Wrap the yarn as tight as you can so everything will hold together. When you reach the bend, pinch the yarn with your finger and thumb so it won't unravel. Then tie the two ends of the yarn together, figure 5-20. If you want, you can dab some glue on the knot to make sure it holds. Trim the yarn ends even, and you have made your own jig.

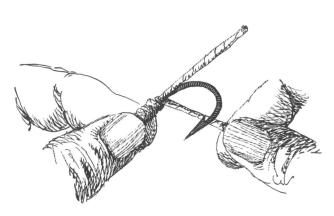

Fig. 5-19

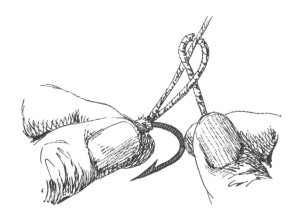

Fig. 5-20

Fig. 5-21

Plastic Worms

You've already learned how to fish with live worms. Believe it or not, you can buy artificial worms, too. They come in many colors: red, blue, yellow, black, brown, green, and even hot pink. Even though they don't look like earthworms, artificial worms catch fish. To make them come alive and attract fish, they need to be moved. To do this, place a split shot ten inches above the plastic worm and retrieve it in as many ways as you would a live worm. One tip, though; they are very attractive bait when fished directly on the bottom.

To hook a plastic worm, tie a large hook to the end of the fishing line and stick the tip of the hook into the worm's head and out the other side. Insert the tip of the hook back into the worm farther down the body, figure 5-21. The tip is put in the body so the hook won't catch on a snag, but will still hook a fish.

Flies

Anglers are deceivers. They deceive the fish into thinking they are being served dinner, when really the fish are the dinner for the anglers. The more difficult the fish is to fool, the greater the reward for the angler. Consider trying to imitate the smallest items in a fish's diet—small insects. Because insects are so numerous and easy to catch, a fish is in no hurry to capture them. The fish takes time to examine the insect before deciding to eat it. Because the fish is so fussy, the artificial fly has to be made just right. It must look like a real insect.

Wherever the fish are feeding, a cast with a good imitation fly holds promise—even if several minutes go by without a bite. Sooner or later a fish will spot your fly and take it. The problem is knowing what insect is on the water and what the fish is eating.

Visit the waters you intend to fish, and observe as much as you can about the insects living there. Note their size, color, and living habits, as well as when and how fish feed on them. With that information you will be able to use feathers, thread, and yarn to make artificial flies that catch fish.

In order to make your own flies, you will need a vise, nylon thread, yarn, small feathers (hackle), a clothespin, and a small pair of scissors.

The vise is used to hold the hook while you are dressing it with the rest of the material. A simple vise can be made from a pair of tweezers, pushed into a hole, drilled in a one-inch thick board. Drill the hole one-half inch from one corner of the board, using a drill bit that is as wide as the metal tweezers.

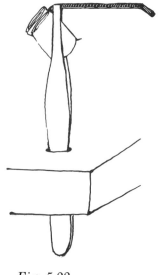

Fig. 5-22

To use the vise, set the board on a table with the hole just over the edge. Place a book on top of the board to steady it. Roll up a three-inch piece of paper, and fold it in half. Pinch the paper on the hook so the point is covered. With the tip of the tweezers, grab the hook just above the paper and push the tweezers down in the hole to squeeze the hook tight, figure 5-22.

Various colored yarns or chenile are materials often used for dressing up the hook. Chenile can be purchased in a sporting goods store, and you might be able to find some yarn around the house. Gray, yellow, brown, red, tan, black, and gray-green are good colors to start with. You will need some very fine nylon thread. Black is the most useful color. A pair of small, pointy-nose scissors is very helpful for cutting the fine thread and trimming the small flies. A hat pin can also come in handy. If a hat pin is not available, use a straight pin, pushed through a small piece of cork. Feathers, or hackle, create the legs of insects and keep dry flies floating on top of the water. You can buy small packages of grizzly hackle from the sporting goods store.

The hooks that fly tiers use are different from bait hooks. They are not as heavy and can be much smaller. They also cost much more than bait hooks. You can use your bait hooks but flatten the little barbs on the shank first.

There are two basic types of flies, dry flies and wet flies. Dry flies float on the water and can represent anything from ants to mayflies. Wet flies sink beneath the surface of the water and can imitate anything from nymphs to minnows.

One fly to tie is called the wooly worm. By changing the color and size and adding or subtracting hackle, the wooly worm can imitate a wide range of insects that fish eat on top and under the water.

To begin your fly tying, use a large size 6 hook. As you tie more flies, you can use smaller ones and make smaller flies. How about starting with a black wooly

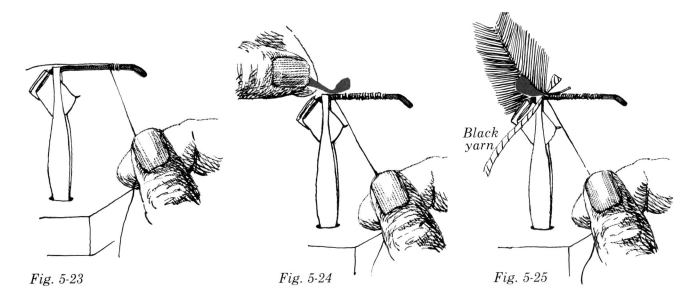

Fig. 5-23

Fig. 5-24

Black
yarn

Fig. 5-25

worm? You will need black chenile or yarn, a small piece
of red yarn, black thread, a three-inch long hackle
feather, and all of the tools already mentioned.

Clamp the hook in your vise with paper at the bend.
Lay the end of a 2-1/2-foot piece of black thread along the
hook shank and wrap the thread over itself to the back
of the hook, figure 5-23. Clip a clothespin to the thread so
it hangs without unraveling. Tie a piece of red yarn on
the back of the hook so it sticks out beyond the bend
about one-fourth inch. Remove the clothespin. Wrap the
thread around the red yarn six or seven times to secure it,
and cut off the extra yarn, figure 5-24. Your wooly worm
now has a tail.

Fasten the end of the black yarn or chenile just in
front of the red tail by wrapping it with the thread. Now
tie on the tip of a hackle feather to the same spot in the
same way, figure 5-25. Continue wrapping the thread all

the way forward to within one-sixteenth inch of the hook eye and clip the clothespin to it again, figure 5-26.

Wind the chenile or yarn tightly forward, figure 5-27, covering the hook completely. Stop winding where the thread stops, and wrap the thread six or seven times around the end of the yarn to hold it. Clip the clothespin back on the thread, and cut off the extra yarn as close to the hook as possible. Your wooly worm now has a body.

Wind the hackle forward over the yarn, spacing the wraps a little, figure 5-28. Stop where the body ends, and wrap it with the thread, too. Once again, put the clothespin back on the thread, and clip off the leftover hackle. Now your wooly worm is wooly.

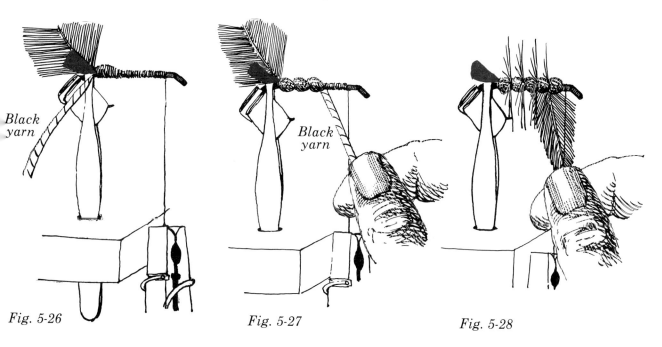

Black yarn

Black yarn

Fig. 5-26   *Fig. 5-27*   *Fig. 5-28*

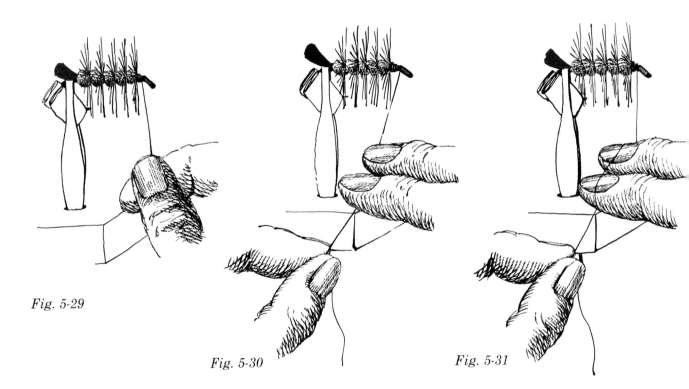

Fig. 5-29

Fig. 5-30

Fig. 5-31

Wrap more thread in between the yarn and eye of the hook to form a head, figure 5-29. To complete the fly, tie three or four half hitches over the head. You tie a half hitch knot by pulling the remaining thread out from the fly, holding it tight with your left hand. Hold two fingers of your right hand out straight and against the thread, figure 5-30. Wrap the thread around the fingers once, forming a loop, figure 5-31. Keeping the thread tight, put the loop over the eye of the hook, removing one finger and placing it on the head of the fly so the loop won't slip off. Now pull the loop closed around the head, figure 5-32. Tying this knot will take a bit of practice, especially keeping the thread tight so it won't unravel, but the half hitch can be mastered. Now dip a pin in a little model airplane glue, and smear it on the head over the knots. Once dry, you can clip the thread off, and your wooly worm is complete, figure 5-33.

You just tied a large, black, wooly worm that can be fished on top or under the water. Check the color and size of the insects at your fishing area, and imitate their size and body color. You can also tie wooly worms to make them float better by putting on thinner bodies and winding the hackle closer together.

The wooly worm and other flies can be fished with a hand line, cane pole, willow pole, spinning outfit, or a regular fly fishing pole. A fly pole is expensive so use whatever you have.

To fish flies on top of the water, use a bobber and no split shot. Regular bobbers will work, but the best kind

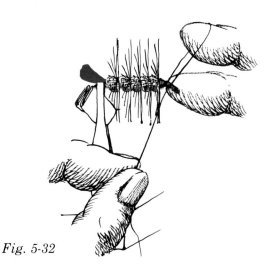

Fig. 5-32

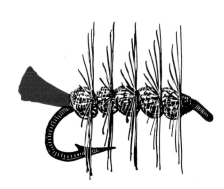

Fig. 5-33

are the clear, plastic ones. They are much less visible and, therefore, less likely to frighten a fish.

It is also important to have a light fishing line so the fish cannot see it. A fish is smart enough to know that a real insect does not have a line attached to it. If your line is large, tie an eighteen-inch piece of small leader to the end (see Appendix: Knots).

Tie the wooly worm to the end of the line (see Appendix: Knots), and put a bobber on twenty inches above the fly. In moving water, cast the fly upstream and let it drift down. Do not pull, move, or change the natural drift of the fly. If you do, the fly will not look natural, and the fish are not likely to strike it.

If you want to fish the wooly worm in deeper water, remove the bobber and add a split shot. Cast upstream, and let the fly drift down. Also, cast across or downstream, and give the fly action by varying the retrieve.

When fishing still water, look for a fish rising to eat insects. A rising fish sometimes comes up fast and makes a good splash, or it might come up slowly, making just a dimple on the surface of the water. Do not cast directly to the place where the fish is eating. The splash of the bobber might frighten the fish. Check the direction the wind is blowing, and cast to one side of the fish, letting the wind blow the fly over it.

When fishing with a cane pole, you can leave the bobber off and just tie the fly to the end of the line. The line should be no longer than the length of the pole. Flip the fly to where you want it on the water, and follow the same steps as you would when using any pole.

When fishing with wet flies, you can leave the bobber on and add a split shot for shallow fishing or remove the bobber for deeper fishing. Try all the different methods used to retrieve other lures. Cast the fly downstream without a bobber, and let it sink to the bottom. Now pull the line up a foot or so, and let it sink back again. Repeat this several times. This action imitates the movement of a nymph underwater. If you catch no fish, try casting to another spot.

As we have said, there are many more fly patterns to try. If you enjoy tying and fishing flies, you can invest a little money and get better tools and more tying material. You must realize, however, that fly tying is a difficult activity that requires patience and skill. The best way to learn to make your own flies is with an experienced fly tier. Fly fishing is a wonderful sport, and many anglers fish no other lure.

CHAPTER 6

Reading Water

Pont and Dare waded a little farther to get into position near a rock, where they saw fish rising. The water was swift and powerful as they moved up and across stream, carefully side stepping like a pair of crabs. Although they were aware that one hasty step would send them splashing downstream, their attention remained on the rock and the fish rising next to it.

The day was a special one for Dare. Pont had come to the city for a visit, and Dare was taking him to his favorite fishing stream. He was anxious to show Pont a good time. Naturally, he wanted to show off a little by proving that he knew as much about fishing his waters as Pont did the streams near his ranch.

Pont was a polite guest and followed Dare's fishing suggestions. After all, they were in Dare's territory. When they arrived at the spot Dare wanted, Pont cast a grasshopper to the rock so it bounced off and into the water. Immediately, he had a strike—a nice twelve incher. That was exactly what Dare had hoped for—a fish for Pont on his first cast. It was the perfect gift for the man who had taught him how to fish. In the half hour that followed, Pont's luck continued.

After catching several fish, Pont, as was his custom,

suggested they let the water "rest." To Pont that meant time to take a nap. They retreated to shore and lay down in the shade of the trees. It was a long half hour for Dare, with lots of grass pulling and rearranging his tackle box before Pont finally stopped snoring.

"The water should be good and rested now," Dare teased, as Pont sat up.

With a yawn, Pont answered, "Yes, I bet it is. I think this time I'll try the little slick just in front of us." Puzzled, Dare watched as Pont waded into the calm area and cast his grasshopper above the slick. What was he up to, Dare wondered? When nothing happened, Pont tried again. After several drifts and still nothing, he pulled in his line and pinched on a split shot. Pont cast his line out to the same spot.

"I never caught anything there before," said Dare, hoping to ease his friend's failure. Pont's line suddenly straightened, and Dare watched in amazement as Pont pulled a seventeen-inch trout to shore.

Pont looked at Dare and smiled. "There is a big difference," he said, "between fishing where you see fish, and fishing by reading the water."

Pont was right. There are some people who have fished a place for many years and have learned where the fish are. These anglers, fishing on strange water, however, would have trouble catching fish because of not knowing where to look. These people could also have trouble on familiar water because no one can always rely on catching fish where one has caught them before.

Some anglers are fish watchers. They watch the water to see a fish either rise or move around, and then go fishing for that fish like a pike after a minnow. Such anglers will catch fish but will miss many more.

The angler who can approach a strange body of water and "read" it is the person who will catch the most fish. Reading water means looking at the water, knowing what fish need to live, and fishing the places where you find those things. Such an angler will always be able to catch fish, even in strange waters.

Different fish live in different places and have different needs. But all fish have a common need for oxygen, the right temperature, protection from enemies and the weather, and food. With these things in mind, an angler can read the water.

The oxygen supply is as important to fish as it is to humans. On a clear, cool, spring day when the air is fresh, you can run, jump, and play all day long. But in a hot, stuffy classroom where fresh air is lacking, sometimes it is difficult to stay awake. The fish are affected the same way. If there is a lot of oxygen in the water, they are active and hungry; when there is less oxygen, they are sleepy and lazy and have no appetite. Thick ice and pollution are two causes of low oxygen levels in water.

In streams and rivers, the moving water is continually refilled with oxygen. The bubbles formed when water pours over rocks help dissolve oxygen into the water. Therefore, when reading moving water, there is no need to worry about oxygen.

The oxygen in ponds and lakes, however, varies with the depth of the water. Generally, the deeper down, the less oxygen there is, and the fewer fish there will be. This is not always true, of course. When it is very hot outside, the warmed water near the surface cannot hold as much oxygen, and the fish will lie deeper. In lakes and ponds another thing to consider is the inflow of moving water. Where a stream or a river flows into a lake, the oxygen level will be higher, and the fish will gather there.

Most fish prefer a certain water temperature. You will find out more about what temperature each type of fish prefers in the next chapter. A general rule of thumb, however, is that a cold water fish will behave sluggishly or even die in warm water. The same is true of a warm water fish in cold water. Knowing the temperature of the various depths in a lake will help you to know how deep to set your line for a particular type of fish. Knowing the water temperature will also help you to choose when to fish. For example, when the temperature of the air begins to cool the water, the once sluggish fish will regain their appetite and become active again. Also, when the temperature is warm, fish will seek cool places to live. They will move to shady places or near inlets of cold streams as well as into deeper water. Often on a sunny day, fish will become active when clouds blow over, cutting down the light and, therefore, cooling the water. The same thing happens when the wind blows across the water, cooling the surface water. That is why early morning, evening, and cloudy days are good times to fish.

Fish also like to have some protection. In streams, fish need protection from the current. Fish cannot swim for long in strong current. Instead, they find a quiet place out of the current to live.

The most obvious, calm place in moving water is a pool. That's why everyone and their Uncle Harry fishes there. Anything interfering with the current can create a calm area. A fallen tree, a rock, or a bridge will have an area of quiet water behind it where fish can live. Objects can also be completely underwater and still slow the current. These places are harder to find but worth looking for.

Fish also hide in places where the current runs slower. The edge of a stream, an undercut bank, steep banks, bends in the stream, and deep runs are all places where the water is slowed enough so the fish are comfortable. Hints can often be seen on the surface. Examples are a smooth area of water that is different from the wavy water around it, or a slow area of current next to fast water. Anglers who are able to find these places are the people who will catch a lot of fish.

In still water, fish also need protection from their enemies and from the weather. Fish will often live in a place where there is a nearby escape route to deeper water. Places such as steep banks, underwater drop-offs, ledges, submerged islands, rock fills, and dams provide excellent escape routes. Weeds and tangles are also great places for fish to hide. Remember, fish like to position themselves where they cannot be seen or next to some object where they are not exposed to danger. Find places to fish where the fish find the greatest protection. Sometimes these places are the hardest to get to, but these spots often house the biggest fish. With a hand line and worms stuffed in your pockets, the only thing you have to worry about getting tangled is yourself—a small matter for a real angler!

The last item that fish need is also the most important. Fish must eat. In looking for food, fish will often be found outside their usual hiding spots. A fish that normally hides next to a stump will swim out into open water to find a meal. A fish in moving water that waits for food to float by its hiding place will leave its area if there is a large insect hatch nearby.

Knowing where to look for fish is one thing; approaching a stream or pond without scaring the fish is quite another. If you go to a lot of trouble to find a place, you certainly don't want to ruin it by being clumsy. Each step you take in or out of the water makes a noise and vibrates the ground. These vibrations are carried through the water. In water, sound travels five times faster than in air so noise really gets around. When a fish senses any strange noises, it gets spooked and is alert to danger. When a fish is spooked, it is next to impossible to catch. Lucky for anglers that a fish has a short memory. It forgets all about the danger in twenty minutes. That is what Pont meant by "resting the water." It is simply letting the fish forget you are trying to catch them. The best thing, of course, is not to frighten them at all.

Whenever you approach the water, don't go running right up to the edge. Instead, tiptoe quietly so the fish will not know you are there. Normal, quiet talking is okay. Those sounds will bounce off the water and not disturb the fish. Loud noises, on the other hand, act like an alarm, warning the fish that danger is near.

Don't cast shadows on the water. Any unusual sight will frighten fish as easily as sound. If you can see the fish, chances are the fish can see you, too. Fish in moving water swim facing upstream. Stay behind them and out of sight. In still water, many fish come to shallow areas looking for food. Again, be sure to stay well back out of sight. Let the moment they take your bait be a big surprise for them.

There are other things about fishing that you can only learn from experience. Some oldtimers have a feel for fishing that comes from years of experience. You're new at fishing, and the only remedy for being a greenhorn is to fish your way out of it.

CHAPTER 7
Fish

Dare was certain everyone on shore could see his red face. He did not think of himself as a poor fisherman, and yet he was being outfished by his cousin Adrian. There he was stuck in the middle of the lake with most of his carefully made lures lying in a heap in the bottom of the boat. What had gone wrong?

There were several nice fish on their stringer, but they were all hers. He thought he could hide his disappointment behind a smile. But when she offered to let him use her gear, his smile melted like a snowball in a frying pan. He wished he was home. He wished he was at school. He wished he was anywhere but in that boat. How could things go so badly?

The morning had started off well. He had even hooked the first fish. But that was the end of his good fortune. When he had the fish close to the boat and reached down to pick it up by the jaw, he saw only the gaping mouth and sharp teeth of the pike. It snapped at him, and pulling his hand back quickly, Dare yanked the fish out of the water. The pike broke free, sending Dare sprawling backwards. From that moment, he had nothing but bad luck. He watched as Adrian hooked pike after pike and lifted them into the boat.

Dare hooked a second fish, but the situation only grew worse. As he was carefully playing the fish, his reel fell off. He hadn't realized the sliding, ring reel holders on his rod were not appropriate for such large fish. Frantically, he grabbed for the reel and caught it. But while he was fumbling to get the reel back on the rod, the pike broke off. Dare slumped to the bottom of the boat. There he sat trying to secure his reel to his rod with Band-Aids.

Had Dare known more about pike, that they are a large, toothy, mean fish, he could have prepared better for the day's fishing. As it was, he learned about pike the hard way. You, too, will learn some things the hard way. Every fishing trip will not be perfect; luck changes with the wind, but not the fun of fishing.

This chapter will provide you with additional information about the more common types of freshwater fish that are found throughout the United States. This information should help you avoid some of the fishing mistakes that Dare made.

Largemouth Bass

The largemouth bass is a hearty fish, native to American waters and lives in just about every state. It is found in warm waters in the sixty-to-eighty degree range but can survive temperatures up to ninety degrees. In the winter when water temperatures drop to fifty degrees, the largemouth will become inactive and stop feeding.

Largemouth bass like to live in slow moving rivers, backwaters, weedy, mud-bottomed lakes, ponds, and in some canals. Generally, they are found in shallow, weedy areas near the surface and down to a twenty foot depth. During hot weather, they will seek cooler waters at greater depths. They like hiding out on the weedy bottom because the fish they eat hide there as well. Fish for them in the morning and evening.

Bass will eat almost anything, but their favorite food is small fish. You can also catch them on worms, large insects, frogs, salamanders, crayfish, and cut up fish. They will strike lures, too, such as spoons, spinners, plugs, plastic worms, jigs, and large, bushy flies.

Smallmouth Bass

The smallmouth bass is much like its cousin, the largemouth, and is found in most North American waters. This bass likes a sixty-to-eighty degree range but cannot live in very warm water. Unlike the largemouth, it remains active in cold winter waters.

The smallmouth likes to live in clear, cool waters of fast flowing rivers and in rocky lakes. It especially likes rocky bottoms in water to a twenty-five foot depth, with deeper drop-offs close by. Normally, the smallmouth does not live below forty feet.

A smallmouth bass eats the same things as a largemouth and can be caught on the same baits and lures.

Walleye

The walleye, which lives mainly in the northern states, received its name from its large eyes, which have a cloudy, blind look. The walleye can see perfectly well, though, and lives in large, clear, cold lakes and rivers. Another fish that lives in schools, the walleye likes to stay in deep water near a rock, gravel, or sand bottom.

This toothy fish eats small fish more than anything else. Minnows make the best bait. They will also bite worms, crayfish, hellgrammites, frogs, salamanders, and cut up fish. A spoon fished deep works very well, and a worm added to it is even better. Spinners and plugs will also catch these fish.

Northern Pike

A northern pike is found only in the northern part of the United States. Other fish closely related to the pike are the pickerel and the giant muskellunge, or musky. The pike prefers cool waters. When the water temperature gets as high as sixty or seventy degrees, a pike becomes sluggish and will not eat.

A pike is a shallow water fish, hiding near weeds, logs, and stumps in large rivers and medium-sized lakes. This fish swims alone and will travel all over a lake, looking for food.

A northern pike will eat anything that moves on or in the water. Its large mouth and razor-sharp teeth allow a pike to feast on large portions. Fish are the pike's favorite food. A northern pike will lie quietly in the weeds, waiting for an unsuspecting fish to swim by. Then the pike will burst from its hiding place and gobble

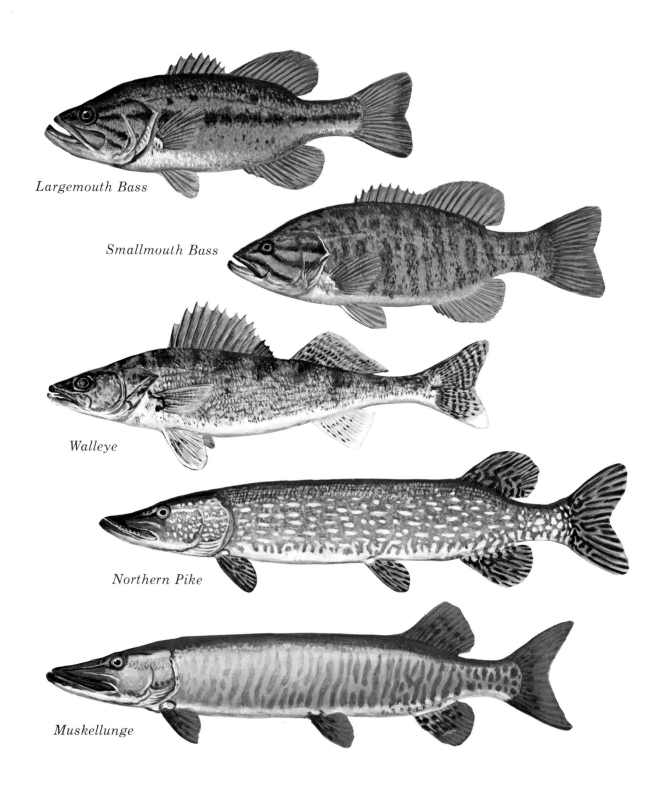

Largemouth Bass

Smallmouth Bass

Walleye

Northern Pike

Muskellunge

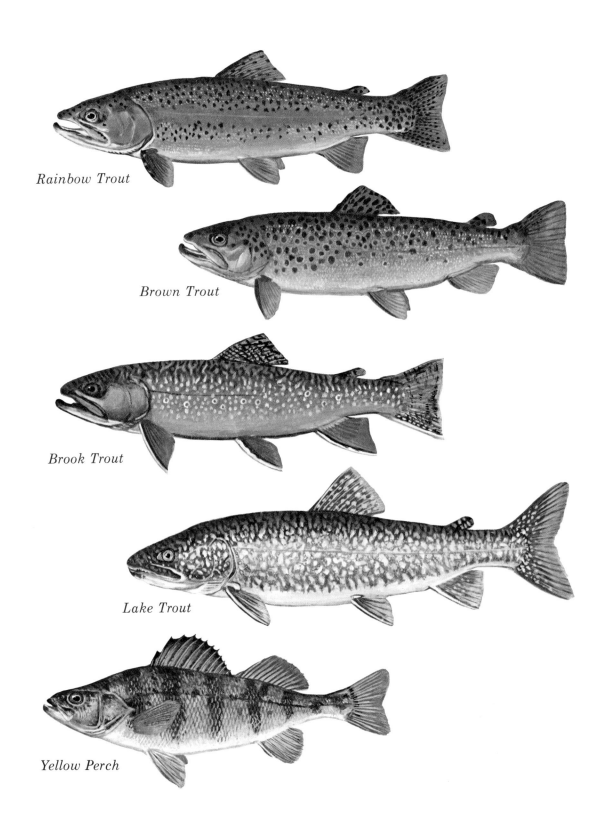

Rainbow Trout

Brown Trout

Brook Trout

Lake Trout

Yellow Perch

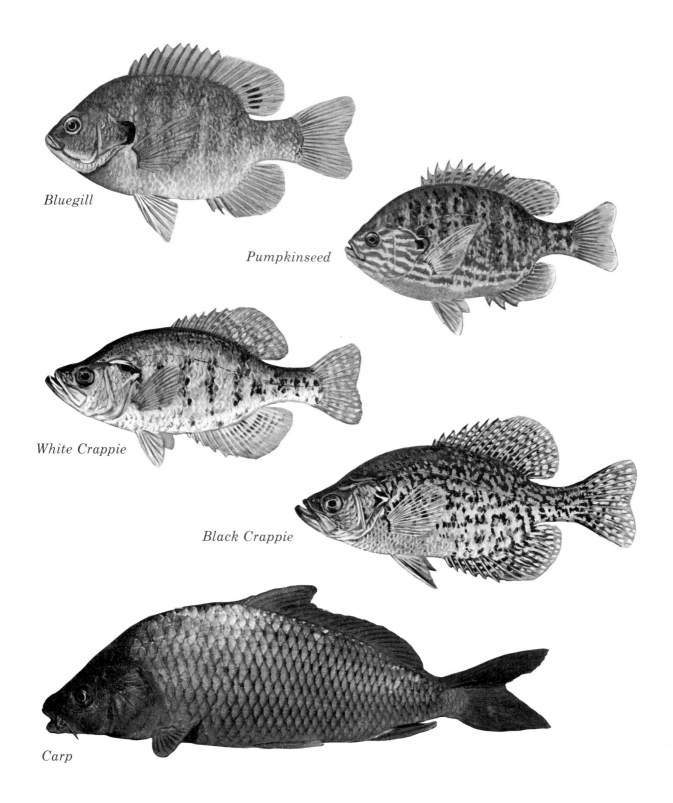

Bluegill

Pumpkinseed

White Crappie

Black Crappie

Carp

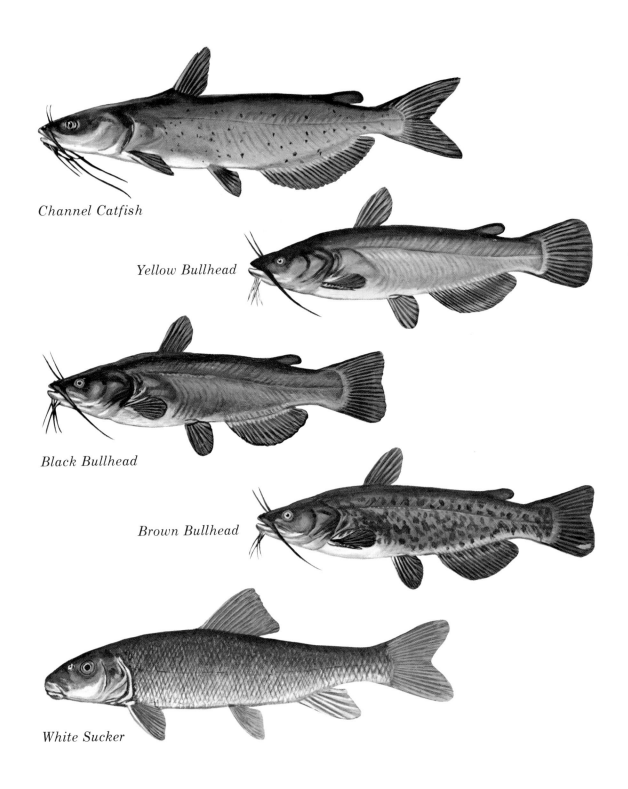

Channel Catfish

Yellow Bullhead

Black Bullhead

Brown Bullhead

White Sucker

up the fish. Use large minnows, worms, crayfish, frogs, and cut up fish for bait. Large floating or diving minnow plugs, spoons, spinners, jigs, and even plastic worms will attract this large fish.

Rainbow Trout

The rainbow, the most common trout, is a fierce fighter. Its cousins include the smaller brook trout, the clever brown trout, the colorful cutthroat, California's golden trout, the huge lake trout, and the Dolly Varden. Most trout are found in clear mountain rivers and lakes. Cold water is what they prefer.

A rainbow will take a wide range of baits: worms, minnows, grasshoppers, crayfish, caterpillars, grubs, fish eyes, cheese, salmon eggs, corn, marshmallows, hellgrammites, and many other water insects. Its big appetite makes spinners, spoons, flies, and plugs all good lures to catch trout.

Yellow Perch

The yellow perch can be found in lakes, ponds, and some slow streams all over North America. Although able to survive a wide range of temperatures, the perch prefers fifty to sixty degrees and can survive very low oxygen levels. A yellow perch lives in schools. It likes to live on the bottom of clear, shallow water near weeds.

When it comes to baits, the yellow perch is not very particular. It will take minnows, worms, crayfish, snails, fish eyes, grubs, grasshoppers, crickets, and small

A rainbow trout caught on a willow pole is something to boast about.

insects. As for lures, the yellow perch will strike jigs, small spinners with a worm on it, and flies.

Bluegill
From sea to shining sea, the bluegill is one of the most popular game fish. It is also the most common of the sunfish, but you may catch the green sunfish, the colorful pumpkinseed, the redear sunfish of the South, the spotted sunfish, the little longear sunfish, or the redbreast sunfish of the East, too. The bluegill and most other sunfish can survive a wide range of temperatures from the very cold to the very warm, though sixty degrees is preferred. Even though they can survive in cold water, bluegills will not eat in cold water. Bluegills cannot handle low oxygen in the water.

Bluegills like to live in quiet, weedy streams and ponds. They can also be found in large lakes, provided there are areas with weeds and deep escape holes nearby. Water from five to fifteen feet deep is their usual dwelling place. They live in schools, so if you catch one fish, you can be sure there are more.

These little fish have great appetites and fight like fish twice their size. Catch them using a worm, cricket, grub, mealworm, caterpillar, or small insects. They will also strike small spinners, jigs, and flies.

Crappie
Crappie are the largest of the sunfish and are caught almost anywhere in the United States. There are two

kinds of crappie: the black crappie usually lives in the North and likes cooler, clear water; the white crappie likes the murky bayous, lakes, and sluggish rivers of the South. Sometimes both types of crappie will be found living in the same water.

Black and white crappies live in schools and feed in the cool of the morning and evening. Weedy areas are their favorite feeding places. They like the shallows, but the heat of the day often drives them deeper. Take care when fishing for crappie; their mouths are tender, and a hook can easily be torn from them.

Crappies love to eat little minnows. They will also eat worms, grasshoppers, crickets, grubs, mealworms, caterpillars, and other insects. The lures they strike most often are yellow and white jigs, spinners, small spoons, and flies.

Carp

Carp are found in most waters in the United States. They prefer warmer ponds, lakes, and rivers of any size. They like the water murky. If introduced into clear water, carp soon muddy the water with their rooting habits. Because of this and the fact that they carry disease and parasites and eat the eggs of other fish, carp are harmful to game fish.

They are listed here because they have made a permanent place for themselves in our waters, and you are likely to catch them. Never throw carp back into the water. Use them for cut bait or garden fertilizer.

You can catch carp with just about anything, although worms, dough balls, cheese, corn kernels, and marshmallows seem to work best. There is even a chance you could catch them on a lure.

Channel Catfish

There is hardly a place in this country where channel catfish cannot be found. Channel catfish have a spine on their back and two poison spines in the fins on their sides. Being stuck by a spine will cause a little pain, so be careful when you handle them. Channel catfish like large, warm, sluggish rivers and weedy lakes. They can also be found in cooler, swifter waters with a sand or gravel bottom.

Catfish are normally nocturnal fish, which means they are active at night. Because they swim around in the dark, they have whiskers for feeling and sensing food in the water. These fish travel to shallow water to feed at dusk and stay deep during the daytime. Catfish can be tempted to eat during the day if the bait is near them.

They will eat worms, minnows, crayfish, hellgrammites, salamanders, insects, dough balls, and all of those wonderful stink baits. They will also strike lures, especially if a worm is attached.

Bullhead

Bullheads are another common catfish, found almost everywhere. They like muddy ponds and lakes as well as sluggish rivers. Bullheads stay on the bottom in schools and can live in polluted water. They are also at home in swift, clear brooks.

Like other catfish, bullheads have spines and feed at night. They, too, can be caught during the day if fished deep. Use worms, minnows, crayfish, insects, dough balls, and stink bait. They will even take a spinner or spoon with a worm on it.

Suckers

The name sucker is given to a large number of different kinds of fish found throughout the United States. Suckers get their name because of their pursed, sucking lips. They find their food by smell and feel. Suckers can live in murky waters but prefer cool, clear lakes and rivers with rock, gravel, or sand bottoms.

Suckers are the vacuum cleaners of the fish world with their toothless, suction cup mouths. They swim along the bottom sucking up snails, worms, insects, and algae. In fact, they will inhale just about anything they can fit in their tiny mouths. You'll often catch them while fishing on the bottom for other fish.

Each of the fish discussed here has its special charms for anglers, and each can be an exciting challenge to catch. For further information on fish in your area, check with the local fish and game department.

CHAPTER 8

Keeping and Cleaning Fish

After the fish has made its last run and pulled its last trick, it still isn't caught. The fish must be removed from the water and put on a stringer—not a simple task. Many anglers have hooked a prize and lost it because they didn't know how to land a fish correctly.

Until now, landing a fish meant dragging the fish on shore or lifting it out of the water. But lifting a fish out of the water by the line is a risky method because often a fish will break the line. Grabbing the fish is a much better way to land it.

This method takes a little practice, and you may lose a few fish in the beginning. In the end, however, grabbing a fish will mean keeping the fish you hook. Here's how you grab a fish. When the fish is tired and close to shore, leave a rod's length of line out. Then extend the rod above and behind you, pulling the fish within reach. To grab a slippery fish, put your thumb in its mouth and pinch the lower jaw, figure 8-1. Lift the fish out of the water and over dry land. Before laying the fish down and taking out the hook, put the fish on a stringer so it will not get away.

There are some fish in whose mouths you wouldn't want to stick your fingers. Pike, pickerel, and muskies

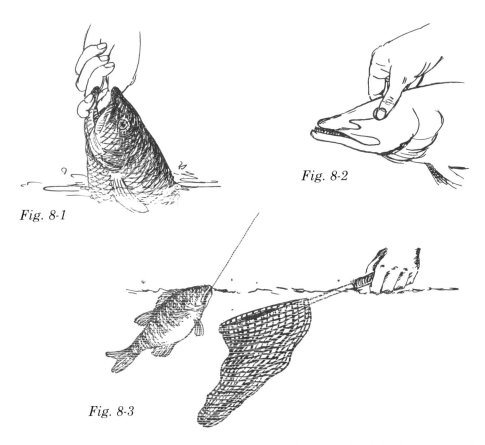

Fig. 8-1

Fig. 8-2

Fig. 8-3

are just such fish. Instead, grab them behind the head on their eyes, figure 8-2. That way you save a fish and your fingers as well.

A net is useful to get fish out of the water when you use it correctly. If you have one, put it in the water and pull the fish over the net. Now lift the net, picking the fish up out of the water with it, figure 8-3.

If the fish is still too wiggly to grab or net when you get it to shore, you haven't let the fish fight long enough to tire itself out. If the fish insists on putting up a fight and you cannot get hold of it, land the rascal any way you can. Once you have the fish on dry land, keep hold of it, or it will wiggle right back into the water.

If the fish is large and too slippery to get a good grip

Landing a fish is exciting, but don't be so excited, like this girl, that you forget to hold on to your fish.

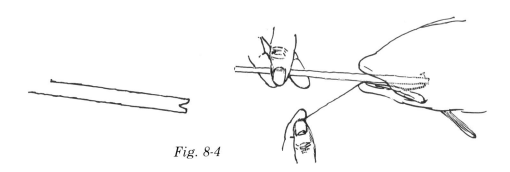

Fig. 8-4

on, rub your hand in the sand. This should give you a good hold on the fish. If your fish is still hard to hold with even a good grip, try flipping the fish on its back. The fish shouldn't be able to move a fin. Get the fish safely on the stringer before removing the hook.

After you land and secure a fish, you might find that the hook has already fallen out, and you'll wonder how in the world you caught it. Most of the time, though, the hook will be set firmly in the jaw or swallowed. You'll need the help of an easily made device to remove the hook. Take a long, narrow, strong stick and saw or carve a slit in one end. Put the slit on the line just inside the fish's mouth, and run the stick down the line until it is stopped by the hook. Push down fairly hard to get the hook out of the fish's flesh. Keeping the fishing line tight, pull stick and hook out together, figure 8-4. If you can see the hook in the fish's mouth, put the stick directly on the hook at its bend and push it out. If the hook is in the lip, it is easiest to push it out with your fingers. You cannot remove a hook by pulling on it. Pulling will only cause the hook to go deeper into the flesh. There will be a time or two when you can't get the hook out. Don't waste good fishing time messing with a hopeless hook. Cut the line and get the hook out when you clean the fish.

There is a good chance that sooner or later something you catch will have to be thrown back because it is illegal to keep. What we mean by illegal is that it is either too small or out-of-season, according to fish and game regulations. There are even some fishing waters where you aren't allowed to keep any fish. In any case, you must know the proper way to release a fish so it will live to fight again.

Try not to remove the fish from the water. A fish can breathe out of water about as well as you can in water. Hold the fish by the jaw and carefully remove the hook. If you know you are going to release the fish, you can make removing the hook easier by flattening or breaking off the barb. If the fish has swallowed the hook whole and is bleeding, the fish will most likely die. If the fish is not injured, don't pull on the hook or try to remove it. Instead, cut the line. The hook won't hurt the fish. A fish produces chemicals that will dissolve the hook.

Once you have removed the hook from the fish or have cut the line, carefully hold the tail with one hand and cradle the fish under the belly with your other hand, figure 8-5. Always handle the fish with wet hands so you

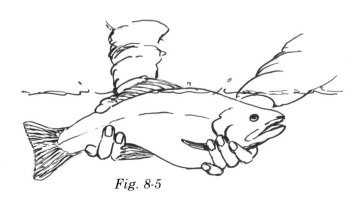

Fig. 8-5

don't wipe off their protective slime. Move the fish back and forth, forcing water into its mouth and out its gills. This helps the fish breathe and recover. If you're in a stream, face the fish into the current but keep it in the slower water. When the fish is ready to swim away, it will move on its own.

Don't squeeze the fish. That will only do harm to its insides. Also, never stick your finger into the gills of fish you intend to release, since doing so will damage it. Finally, never just toss fish back in the water; that is as bad as squeezing them. If you do any of these things, the fish may swim away out of sight. Later, however, you may find it belly up and lying in the water along the shore—good for nothing but bird bait.

Once you've caught your limit, or have decided to quit fishing, you'll need to clean your catch. Cleaning the fish for cooking means removing their insides and, when necessary, scaling them. To remove their insides turn the fish on its back and look for a hole, the anus, near the tail, figure 8-6. Cut a *V* to remove the anal area, and place your knife point into the hole with the cutting edge pointing up. Make your cut down the middle of its belly, the entire length of the fish, using just the tip of the knife blade, figure 8-7. Don't cut too deeply and split the guts. Cut the area between the gills, figure 8-8, grab the gills, and pull down towards the tail of the fish. As you do this, you will pull gills, guts, and all out of the fish. Then if you choose, off with its head and tail!

Cut open the fish's stomach after it has been

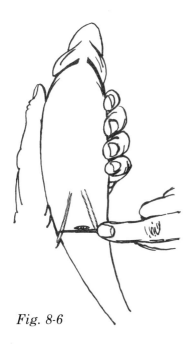

Fig. 8-6

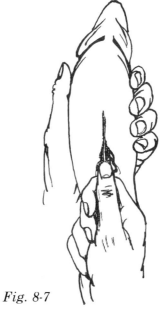

Fig. 8-7

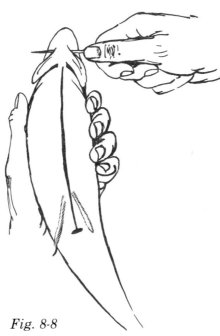

Fig. 8-8

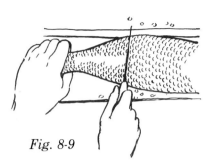

Fig. 8-9

removed to see what the fish has eaten. Knowing this will allow you to use the same bait the fish feed on. Once the guts are out, do not throw the mess onto the shore or into the water. This garbage should be thrown into the trash can. Carry a couple of plastic bags with you to put the guts in.

On the inside of the fish along the back of the body cavity you just opened is a dark blood line. Use your thumb to scrape the blood line out, and then wash the cavity in water. After the fish has been washed, try to keep the fish dry because water will cause fish to spoil. Put your fish in a cooler packed in ice or in a homemade creel, figure 3-13. Either container will keep the fish fresh until you get home.

When you get home your fish will need to be washed again. You might also need to scale the fish before freezing or eating, depending on the type of fish it is. You can feel the scales by rubbing your finger along the side from tail to head. To scale the fish, hold it by the tail on the ground or on a board. Scrape a knife along the side of the fish from tail to head, figure 8-9. As you do, scales will fly off, making a bit of a mess. Scrape each side until all the scales are removed. Rinse the fish in water one more time.

Catfish do not have scales, but they do need to be skinned. To do this cut off the head and gut the fish as

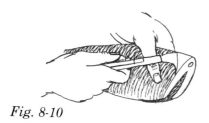
Fig. 8-10

usual. Cut through the skin from the front to the tail, all along the back. Now peel a bit of the skin up so you can get hold of it with a pair of pliers. Pull the skin off slowly towards the tail, figure 8-10. Each side must be done separately. The skin will not come off easily, but with a little work the job will be done.

Whether you decide to eat the fish right away or freeze it for later, you should check to see if it is spoiled. To do this push your finger into the side of the fish. If your finger mark stays, it is probably bad meat. If the flesh is firm and bounces back, the meat is definitely good. Also check the fish's eyes. If they are cloudy, the meat is probably bad.

If you're camping out or just fishing at your favorite spot and you feel like eating a fish or two—go ahead. You're in for a treat. If it is permitted, build a small fire, and burn the wood down to hot coals. Wrap each fish separately in aluminum foil. If you plan ahead, bring along a lemon, tomato, green pepper, and some salt and pepper. Slice the lemon and vegetables, and place them inside the fish with salt and pepper to taste. Plain fish is very good, too. Put the fish wrapped in aluminum foil right on top of the hot coals. Cook a medium fish (twelve inches) for about five minutes on each side. Remove the fish from the fire, and let the foil cool a bit before unwrapping your meal. (The aluminum foil can double as a plate.) The size of the fish determines the length of time needed for cooking. Larger fish should cook longer, while smaller fish need less time. A fish is cooked when the meat is tender and flaky and falls off the bones easily. If the fish is not fully cooked, just wrap it up again and put it back on the coals.

Dare prepared his fish in a very simple but delicious way. He would bring along a frying pan and some bacon. After frying a couple slices of bacon, he would cook the whole fish, without cleaning it, in the bacon grease. When the fish was done, he would peel off the skin and eat the meat off the outside of the bones.

There are many recipes for cooking fish. Look them up in a cookbook, and try what sounds good to you. Cooking your own catch for the family can be fun.

CHAPTER 9

Action by the Water

Water Safety

The accident happened so fast. Dare was wading confidently at the river's edge. Suddenly, he was over his head and swept downstream. He was frightened, but he knew how to handle himself. As Dare fell underwater, he quickly twisted himself so that his feet faced downstream to guard against rocks. He knew that if he hit his head on one he could be knocked unconscious. With his head and feet up and lying on his back, the force of the current would lift him to the surface. Dare fought the natural urge to panic as he was tossed and pushed by the force of the water. He came to the surface and gulped air, but the current hit him, and again he went under. Once more the force of the water carried him to the surface. This time he scraped the bottom and washed into a calm eddy. He put his feet down and stood up. Dare had saved himself.

Dare was relieved to be on firm ground, but as a true angler, he was also relieved that he still had his rod in hand. He had traveled nearly one hundred feet in those few seconds. Like a stick thrown in fast water, the current had swept him off his feet and downstream through a rapids. The same current had popped him to the surface and had deposited him in shallow water.

Rivers can be dangerous for anglers, and Dare was grateful that he knew how to handle himself. He was also ashamed that he had ignored the first rule of fishing—always go fishing with a partner. If he had been in worse trouble, no one would have known; no one would have been able to help. He promised himself that he would not be so foolish again. Make yourself the same promise.

Moving water presents great difficulties, even for good swimmers, but there are ways of saving yourself. If you fall in over your head in a large river, position yourself so you are floating on your back with your feet downstream. When you surface, swim diagonally downstream with the current towards shore. Never try to swim against the current, or you will soon be exhausted.

In smaller, swifter streams, rocks are the major danger. You do not want to bash into them. The best thing to do is to turn yourself so that you float feet first downstream. Shortly, you will either drift towards one shore or the other, or you will find youself at a point in the river where you can stand up and walk out.

Even around still water there is danger. Many ponds and lakes have steep sides that drop off into deep water. These bodies of water can have loose gravel, sand, or even slippery mud at the edges. With these conditions, it is easy to slip into the water and be over your head.

An accident is always a surprise. You must be prepared to act quickly. That means you have to practice having accidents. That's right. Pretend what might happen while fishing. First of all, if you cannot swim, you must learn. In the meantime, wear a life preserver, but don't let the life preserver keep you from learning to swim. Once you know how to swim, practice with your clothes on. If you fish moving water, you must be able to swim in moving water.

Panic is a major factor in most water-related deaths. You have to work at remaining calm because your impulse will be to struggle furiously. You will soon become exhausted and sink. Force yourself to be calm. Keep your head back so it is low in the water to help you float. Don't exhaust yourself struggling. A relaxed body on the surface of the water floats naturally.

You can prevent most accidents by being very careful around water. Never wade deeper than your knees, and always go fishing with someone else. The buddy system will give you a helping hand as well as make fishing more pleasant. If a river is big, swift, and deep, go with an adult. Keep an eye on your buddy, and look out for each other's safety. Above all, learn to swim with your clothes on, and always be prepared for the surprise accident.

Fishing Politely

Rarely will you find yourself and your buddy on a river or pond fishing alone. Instead, you will be spending most of your days fishing where other people are fishing. That is a fact of the sporting life. Any time people are together there is a need for politeness. To have a boat run over

Always go fishing with someone else.

your bobber or a person walk up and start fishing in the same place you are is certainly unpleasant. Crowded fishing conditions can take the fun out of the sport. Here are a few ideas to help you be an angler who is welcome at and can even enjoy a crowded fishing hole.

The best rule is don't do anything that you wouldn't want someone else to do. Don't fish too closely to where someone else is fishing. Twenty-five yards is a good distance. If an area is more crowded, it isn't worth fishing there.

Do not cast where another person's line is already in the water. Let the angler fish that particular spot, and find your own. If you insist on remaining, you could tangle both lines. Often you will be tempted to remain, especially when other people are catching fish, and you are not. Don't be tempted. Remember, too, it could be your line someone casts over!

If you are wading and come onto someone fishing, get out of the water and walk around farther upstream so you do not disturb the fish or the person fishing. Remember that even what you do on shore could scare fish and ruin someone else's fishing.

Don't be noisy, and don't be a nuisance. Quiet fishing catches more fish. Playing, throwing rocks in the water, letting your dog run loose, and wading just for fun do not mix with fishing. Think of the other person first.

Do not litter or leave a mess on shore or in the water. Garbage includes your bait as well as fish guts and orange peels. In fact, leave the place cleaner than you

Find your own spot and fish politely and safely.

found it. A fishing spot should be a joy to come to, not an eyesore.

Be the kind of angler you would like other people to be—thoughtful and courteous. Obey all the fishing regulations. Help your fish and game department with projects such as cleaning up lakes and streams. They need volunteers who are willing to help. Everything they do is designed to make the fishing better.

CHAPTER 10

Life in a Pond

Ecology is the study of the relationship plants and animals have with each other and their surroundings. Each creature, be it grizzly bear, trout, mayfly, or you, needs certain things to survive. Learning what those things are helps us to know when we are doing damage to them. Looking at individual animals won't help much, but studying everything together will.

In a pond, lake, stream, or any natural body of water, there are many forms of underwater life besides fish, and all are important. Sometime when the fish aren't biting, squat down by the water and stare at the mud on the bottom. You will find such places filled with all kinds of weird creatures. Every one, no matter how tiny, ugly, or strange to us, is helping to make that pond a good place to live.

You can have a miniature pond of your own. If you don't have a glass aquarium or a fish bowl, a plastic washtub will work. Put a couple of handfuls of pond mud in the fish bowl with plenty of pond water and a glob of algae or pond weeds. Take your pond home, and let everything settle. There may already be a few things living in there: flatworms, some mites, beetles, and probably some insect larvae. Make a net out of a coat hanger and an old nylon stocking, figure 4-12. Net more insects from the pond to put in your own pond. Catch a few tadpoles, a snail, and anything else that interests you. However, don't catch anything that will eat other pond life. Crayfish and minnows will eat each other and a lot more, too! By observing your homemade pond, you will come to appreciate all that happens in the water where you fish. You will want to protect your fishing spots so everyone can enjoy the life and fishing found there.

By watching your own little pond, you will also begin to understand that everything in the water depends on everything else for food, shelter, and population control. If you look at some pond water under a magnifying glass or a microscope, you will see many tiny creatures swimming around. These small organisms are extremely important to the life of that pond. Some of these creatures may eat plants and are, in turn, eaten by water beetles. The water beetle makes a good meal for a minnow which, in turn, is eaten by our friend, the bluegill. There are lots of different critters that eat plants and are, in turn, eaten by other creatures that feed still other animals, which include game fish. This is all part of the food chain. If too many creatures are removed, the pond can become fishless and dead.

Plants are the beginning of the food chain. Remove the plants, and everything in the pond will starve. If, on the other hand, there were plants but no plant eaters, the plants would grow wild and fill every inch of the pond.

There would be no room for the fish to live, and, therefore, no more fishing.

Remove the meat sourcs, such as the crayfish, from a
pond, and the meat-eating fish would have only each
other to eat. These fish would eat each other right out of
existence. If there were no meat-eating fish, the plant
eaters would grow unchecked. They soon would eat more
plants—maybe all of them. As you can see, everything
depends on everything else to keep the pond alive and
well, maintaining a perfect balance.

Branches and logs also have a place in the pond
although you may not think so after losing some hooks
in them. If they were removed, the fish wouldn't have as
many places to hide. The minnows and the insects that
the fish eat wouldn't have as many places to live and
breed in, so there wouldn't be as many fish in the pond.
Cleaning out the snags would only result in cleaning out
the fish.

You may wonder what effect you are having on the
pond when you catch and keep fish. Will the plants take
over the pond? That is doubtful unless so many fish are
caught that there are too few to do their job. Catching
fish really helps pond life. An angler becomes part of the
pond's ecology by catching fish, which keeps a balance
of fish in area waters. The fish and game department
sets limits on the number of fish you can catch. They
have studied the fish and know how many can be safely
taken out. Obey their regulations.

Some day you might be tempted to introduce your

favorite fish into a pond where it does not exist. That would make the fishing all the more fun, right? Wrong! Let's see what would happen if you put bass in a trout pond. Bass breed faster than trout and have larger appetites. Their food includes small trout. Soon there would be too many bass for the pond, and they could not grow very big. The fishing would be ruined; there would be few trout and lots of tiny bass. That's the reason moving fish from one body of water to another is illegal.

Pollution affects pond life. Polluted water can kill fish, frogs, hellgrammites, and plants. Pollution can take all the oxygen out of the water, and it can be a deadly poison. You would not want to catch and eat fish that live in poisoned water. You can help keep waters clean by not polluting and by helping community or fishing clubs clean up the ponds and streams in your area. The fishing waters in your area are your responsibility; help keep them clean and beautiful.

Erosion can ruin good fishing water. The weeds, brush, and trees lining the banks may make casting difficult, but they do keep the river banks from washing away. Remove them and the first rain will cause the banks to wash into the river, filling it and the lakes below with silt and mud. Silt in the water is not only ugly, but it also clogs up the gills of fish, kills their eggs, and destroys their food supply.

A body of water is a delicate part of nature. It is filled with life, which makes it beautiful as well as abundant with fish. There is only one beast that has the power to keep that beauty or destroy it, and that is us, the people of the earth. Look carefully at the water where you fish. Watch the heron, spearing fish in the shallows. Look at the ducklings, gliding across the water. Listen to the redwing blackbird, singing among the cattails, and watch the muskrat, lazily swimming by. Love the outdoors, be a good caretaker, and have fun fishing.

Catching the Big One

Dare and Billy turned off the street into the alley. At the end of the narrow lane, a dirt road ran behind a junkyard, heading towards the river. This road led to a pond, which had formed in an abandoned gravel pit. Dare and Billy quickened their pace as they approached the pond.

An early morning mist hung over the water as a pair of ducks floated smoothly across the pond. Hidden among the reeds, bullfrogs croaked their morning music.

The two boys walked along a well-worn path on the water's edge, watching for signs of fish. They were amazed by the wild quietness, which surrounded them. There was a strange, exciting feel in the morning air as they headed for their favorite spot, a deep hole bordered on two sides by shallow water, choked with cattails.

As they approached this hole, a frightened frog leaped into the water and swam towards the cattails. Suddenly, a catfish broke the surface, swallowed the frog, and dove out of sight, splashing its tail with a mock wave. The size of the splash meant it was a large catfish, the granddaddy of the pond.

"It's still here," Dare whispered, so excited he could hardly get his knife open to cut a willow pole. "No one has caught it."

All summer this catfish had been stealing their hooks and more worms than they cared to count. The boys always worried that someone else might catch the fish that had so often made fools of them. Dare tied his line to the end of the pole and threaded a worm on the hook.

"I'm going to get him today. That old catfish won't sucker me anymore," Dare whispered to Billy as he flipped the worm into the water.

While Billy and Dare fished, the sun moved high across the sky until it finally dropped behind the trees, covering them in shade. By the end of the day, their stringers were full of fish, but none of them was the granddaddy. They had run out of worms an hour before and were now using whatever they could find for bait. It was time to go home.

Billy yawned and said, "Come on, let's go."

Dare pretended not to hear him. He had found a black salamander under a rotten log and wanted to try it. The very thing to catch that clever fish, he thought. He pulled in his line, hooked on the salamander, and cast it out into the deep hole.

"Come on, let's go," Billy pleaded, gathering up his gear. "It's getting dark."

"Just a minute," answered Dare. His hope for catching the granddaddy was in this one last try.

Dare's shoulders drooped as he began pulling in the line. When he thought his line snagged, his disappointment turned to anger. He gave the line a terrific yank. To his surprise, his line pulled and jerked in return, bending his pole almost to the breaking point. Suddenly, a catfish surfaced, thrashing wildly, and Dare knew he had hooked the giant. He ran up the bank, whooping with delight, and pulled the fish onto the shore.

Dare and Billy couldn't believe their eyes. On the muddy bank lay the great fish, the granddaddy of the pond. Dare picked it up. Without a doubt, this catfish was a record.

"Wow!" Dare said in a hushed voice. "Will this impress everyone at home. We could even get it mounted."

But somehow he wasn't as happy as he thought he would be. He stood quietly for a second, looking around. He saw the bright blaze of the sunset cast a fading orange light on the pond. The trees stood silent now without the wind to move them. Before him, the catfish lay struggling for its life. Without saying a word, Dare gently put the fish back into the water and watched as it swam away. Billy's mouth dropped open in disbelief.

Dare shrugged. "The pond just wouldn't be the same without it," he said, with a sigh.

One Last Word

As you can see, fishing is really a simple sport, requiring little but giving much in return. The pleasure is doubled when one loves the sport enough to want to make it pleasant for others and when one appreciates the fish and the places fish live.

Lack of equipment is no reason to miss the fun of fishing. Indeed, finding and making fishing equipment is an important part of the adventure. All you really need is the interest and the desire. We have tried to provide the rest. In doing so, we hope to have gained many more fishing companions. At the same time, we expect to find more fish and see more beautiful surroundings because of your interest and efforts. Say hello if you should ever meet us on the water. We'll ask you how the fishing is and wish you good luck. Oh yes, if you happen to see Dare, ask him about that catfish.

Appendix: Knots

The knots presented in this section are common to anglers and will be useful in most fishing situations.

Clinch Knot

A clinch knot is used for tying hooks or lures to the end of the fishing line. To tie a clinch knot, begin by putting the line through the eye of the hook, figure A-1. Twist the end of the line five or six times around itself and thread it back through the loop near the hook eye, figure A-2. Now pass the line through the second loop and pull tight. Clip off the short end of the line that sticks out, figure A-3.

The clinch knot can also be used for tying string to a pop tab and wire to a stringer. It is also good for tying nylon or waxed string to a casting stick, cane pole, or willow pole. Be sure to notch the end of these items so the line will not slip off.

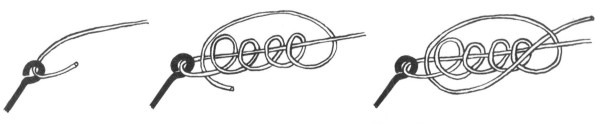

Fig. A-1   *Fig. A-2*   *Fig. A-3*

Blood Knot

The blood knot is used for tying two pieces of nylon fishing line together. To do this twist one line three or four times around the other and pass that line through the loop formed by the crossing of the lines, figure A-4. Twist the second line around the first three or four times in the opposite direction and pass it through the loop, too, figure A-5. Pull all four ends of the line tight and cut off the short ends, figure A-6.

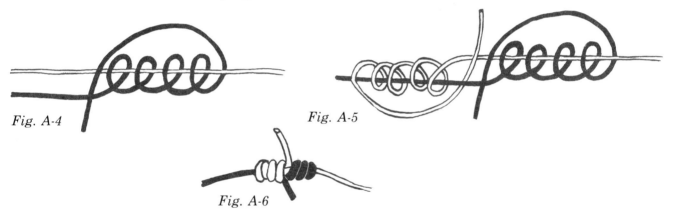

Fig. A-4   *Fig. A-5*

Fig. A-6

Reel Knot

The reel knot is a simple knot used for tying the end of the line to the reel spool. Loop the line around the spool, and tie a simple overhand knot around the line. Tie another overhand knot on the end of the line to keep the first knot from slipping, figure A-7. Pull the long portion of the line until the knot is snug on the spool.

Fig. A-7

Dropper Knot

When you want to have more than one hook on your line, or you are fishing a stream and need a place to attach a weight, the dropper is the knot to use. It is simply a blood knot with one end left long, figure A-8. You can get the same result tying clinch knots to a three-way swivel or to a button, figure A-9.

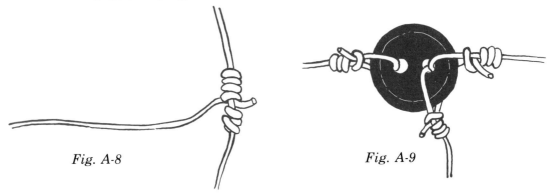

Fig. A-8   Fig. A-9

Bowline Knot

If you are using waxed string for fishing line, you'll probably want to have a nylon leader to tie the hook or lure to. You can tie string and nylon together by making a bowline knot on the end of the string. Start the bowline by making a small loop near the end of the line through which you should pass the end of the line, figure A-10. Pass the end around the string and back through the small loop while pulling the small loop tight, figure A-11. Tie the nylon leader to the loop with a clinch knot, figure A-12.

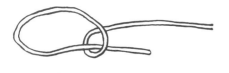

Fig. A-10

Fig. A-11

Fig. A-12

Glossary

angler—a person who tries to catch fish with a hook and bait

artificial lure—a device used to catch fish; a bait made from wood, metal, fur, or feathers that looks like the food fish eat

backwater—a stretch of still or slow moving water, joining a stream

bail wire—a heavy wire on the front of an open face reel that keeps the line from unraveling until you cast

bait—the food fish like to eat, which is placed on a hook and used to attract fish

bayou—a marshy inlet or very slow moving creek

bite—the act of a fish taking a bite of bait from a hook

bobber—a device used to keep fishing line and bait floating on or near the surface of the water; also a float

creel—a bag or basket used to store and transport fish

downstream—in the direction the river or stream is flowing

drag—a device on a fishing reel that determines how hard or easy it is to pull line out

drift—a method of fishing in which you let the bait and line move freely with the flow of the stream

eddy—a place on a river where water swirls around in the opposite direction the river is flowing

fish hatchery—special farms where fish are hatched and raised

float—a device used to keep fishing line and bait floating on or near the surface of the water; also a bobber

fly—an artificial lure made of a hook, fur, and feathers to imitate insects

hackle—the feathers of certain kinds of fowl, usually chickens, which are used in making artificial flies

insect hatch—an insect larva hatching from an egg underwater, swimming to the surface, and flying away

jig—an artificial lure with a lead head

larva—the youthful stage in the growth of an insect when it is coming out of the egg; also a nymph

leader—a thinner, less visible, short section of fishing line tied between the hook and the heavier, main portion of the fishing line

lure—an object used to attract and catch fish, usually attached to a hook

nymph—the youthful stage in the growth of an insect; also larva

planter—a fish that has been raised in a hatchery and put in lakes and streams for anglers to catch

playing the fish—the act of allowing a fish to run until it is tired

plug—an artificial lure made from wood to look like a fish

retrieve—the act of pulling fishing line or lure through the water in such a way as to entice the fish to bite

roe cluster—the bag of eggs found in female fish

sinker—a weight used to sink a fishing line

slick—a smooth looking, calm area on the surface of a stream, caused by a hidden rock or log

slough—a shallow, weedy body of water, lying just off a river or lake

snag—an underwater object, usually a tree or weed, that catches or tangles your hook and line

snap swivel—a device attached between the end of the line and the lure that turns with the lure to keep the line from becoming twisted

spinner—an artificial lure with a blade, which spins around when pulled through the water

split ring—a ring for connecting hooks to lures

split shot—a round weight with a slit for pinching it on fishing line

spoon—a spoon-shaped artificial lure made of metal

strike—a hard and sudden bite by a fish

stringer—a string or stick used to hold live fish in the water after they have been caught

upstream—in the opposite direction the river or stream is flowing

weight—a small, lead ball used to sink a fishing line; also a sinker

Index

Charles and George Roberts learned to fish in a large city where they grew up, but since then they have fished throughout North America. "This book," say the authors, "fills the modern need of young people who have no adult to teach them fishing. It gives young people a chance to start simply and grow with the sport rather than thrusting them into situations where fishing is more expensive and complicated than fun."

Charles Roberts is a surveyor for the U.S. Forest Service in Idaho's Nez Perce National Forest. His brother George is an associate professor of art at Boise State University, where he teaches drawing, printmaking, and design. Charles currently resides in Grangeville, Idaho, while George lives in Boise with his wife and three daughters.